Praise for

The *Books of Awesome*
and Neil Pasricha

"Strangely heartwarming . . . perfect for rainy days."

The New Yorker

"Sunny without being saccharine, it's a countdown of life's little joys that reads like a snappy Jerry Seinfeld monologue by way of Maria von Trapp."

Vancouver Sun

"Laugh-out-loud funny, tinged with just enough sarcastic nostalgia."

Wired

"Neil Pasricha is the guru of small joys."

Toronto Star

"Neil Pasricha makes ordinary days light up with awesomeness."

Gretchen Rubin

"Pasricha provides a contemporary take on everyday inspiration that skips the typical Chicken Soup for the Soul fare. . . . Though tongue-in-cheek, Pasricha emerges a committed but inviting optimist, combating life's unending stream of bad news by identifying opportunities to 'share a universal high five with humanity.'"

Publishers Weekly

"Celebrates and honors the little joys of life!"

USA Today

"Laugh-out-loud. You will feel like you've thought of these things a thousand times but just haven't stopped to write them down."

BBC South America

"It's nice to remind yourself of life's sweeter side and the pleasures to be had from the small things—like peeling the thin plastic film off new electronic gadgets and sneaking your own cheap snacks into the cinemas. Life really is awesome after all."

The Guardian

"Neil Pasricha tops the list of awesome."

The Globe and Mail

Our

Book

of

Awesome

A Celebration of the Small Joys
That Bring Us Together

Neil Pasricha
and friends

Published by Simon & Schuster

New York   London   Toronto   Sydney   New Delhi

SIMON &
SCHUSTER
CANADA

Simon & Schuster Canada
A Division of Simon & Schuster, Inc.
166 King Street East, Suite 300
Toronto, Ontario M5A 1J3

This Simon & Schuster Canada edition December 2022

Illustrations by Monsieur Cabinet

SIMON & SCHUSTER CANADA and colophon are
trademarks of Simon & Schuster, Inc.

For information about special discounts for bulk purchases, please contact Simon &
Schuster Special Sales at 1-800-268-3216 or CustomerService@simonandschuster.ca.

Manufactured in the United States of America

1   3   5   7   9   10   8   6   4   2

Library and Archives Canada Cataloguing in Publication

Title: Our book of awesome : a celebration of the small
joys that bring us together / Neil Pasricha.
Names: Pasricha, Neil, author.
Identifiers: Canadiana (print) 2022026208X | Canadiana (ebook) 20220262098
| ISBN 9781982164508 (hardcover) | ISBN 9781982164515 (ebook)
Subjects: LCSH: Conduct of life—Humor. | LCSH: Conduct of
life—Anecdotes. | LCGFT: Humor. | LCGFT: Anecdotes.
Classification: LCC PN6231.C6142 P375 2022 | DDC 818/.602—dc23

ISBN 978-1-9821-6450-8
ISBN 978-1-9821-6451-5 (ebook)

Being so obsessed with books you read every single word on the copyright page?
AWESOME!

Our

Book

of

Awesome

So what's this all about?

In my late twenties my wife left me and my best friend took his own life. I couldn't eat, I couldn't sleep, and I lost forty pounds due to stress. I started going to therapy twice a week and began a blog to try and cheer myself up. The blog was called *1000 Awesome Things* and for the next 1000 straight weekdays I posted a short essay about one small joy in life.

My mind was dark and many of my attempts were duds— my first awesome thing was broccoflower, the "strange mutant hybrid child of nature's ugliest vegetables"—but some posts started finding a nerve. Warm underwear out of the dryer, the smell of bakery air, when cashiers open new checkout lanes at the grocery store, getting called up to the dinner buffet first at a wedding, and playing on old, dangerous playground equipment. (Who else remembers burning hot slides?)

Still, nobody read the blog except for my mom. Although, one day, she forwarded it to my dad and my traffic doubled. And then one day I started getting tens of hits. And then one day I started getting hundreds. And then thousands. And then . . . millions. It just got bigger and bigger and bigger and bigger and then I got a phone call and the voice on the other end of the line said, "You just won the Best Blog in the world award!"

And I said, "That sounds totally fake."

But turns out it was real. It was the International Academy of Digital Arts and Sciences and they flew me down to New

York City to parade me down a red carpet before handing me the award for "Best Blog" in the world. When I got home to Toronto I found ten literary agents waiting for me in my inbox, eager to turn *1000 Awesome Things* into . . . *The Book of Awesome.*

The Book of Awesome came out in 2010 and landed on the *New York Times* bestseller list and stayed on international bestseller lists for over 200 weeks. Over the next two years a litany of sequels and spinoffs followed: *The Book of (Even More) Awesome, The Book of (Holiday) Awesome, The Calendar of Awesome, The Journal of Awesome, The App of Awesome*, and on it went.

The book spawned a pre–social media movement of people mailing in photos of themselves with the book in front of famous landmarks and hundreds of elementary and high schools creating plays, projects, and homemade *Books of Awesome* based on the concept. I was invited to give a TED Talk, got asked to "teach America to be happy" on the *Today* show, and was flown to Abu Dhabi to speak to the royal family.

It was an overwhelming couple of years. Through it all, I was driving to my nine-to-five job at Walmart every day, going to therapy twice a week, and feeling pretty lonely in my tiny bachelor apartment downtown. I also felt destabilized by the newfound visibility and pressure, so two years after *The Book of Awesome* came out . . . I stopped. It was painful but I stopped writing the blog, stopped writing sequels, and finally started realizing how depleted I was inside. I knew something was missing.

After hundreds of bad dates over the next couple years, I

met and fell in love with a woman named Leslie, an inner-city elementary school teacher in the Toronto public school board. After a year of dating we moved in together, and then a year after that I got down on one knee and asked her to marry me. She said yes.

Over the next few years, my writing went to new places. After Leslie told me she was pregnant on the flight home from our honeymoon, I started writing a 300-page love letter to our unborn child about how to live a happy life. That letter became *The Happiness Equation: Want Nothing + Do Anything = Have Everything*. After struggling with overwhelm and mental disorganization I created a daily journal to help myself called *Two-Minute Mornings*. After getting addicted to social media and late-night scrolling I started a podcast called *3 Books* to help me reprioritize reading in my life. And after years suffering with low confidence, low resilience, and thin skin, even despite my perceived success, I wrote a book called *You Are Awesome: How to Navigate Change, Wrestle with Failure, and Live an Intentional Life*. I continue, or hope to continue, to keep exploring other themes under the big question of how we live our most intentional lives.

So now, more than ten years after *The Book of Awesome*, why write another? Why return to that old and tired concept? Is this a desperate cash grab? A response to a viral online campaign? A guy completely out of ideas? No, no, and I hope not.

To be honest, I just . . . needed it. My brain needed awesome things again. Over the past few years, I've found myself feeling overwhelmed by a world that seems messed up with algorithm-infused addictions, widening wealth gaps, destabilizing senses of reality, reductions in privacy and freedoms—all against a backdrop of environmental, political, and mental health turmoil. I have felt raw, fried, chewed up, and spit out, and so I have turned to the medicine that works for me. Finding small pleasures. Writing them down. Focusing on gratitude. Soaking into the endless simple joys we're surrounded by every day.

Sure, yes, I know the research: writing down gratitudes improves our mindset, helping us to be positive. But who cares about the research? What truly matters is how we feel. *The Book of Awesome* was never designed to be a prescriptive toolkit teaching you how to find gratitudes. Rather, it's meant to bathe us all in a big awesome pool and maybe offer us an awesome lens so we might sharpen the same seeing skills ourselves.

What makes something awesome? Awesome things can be simple, free, universal, snappy, idiosyncratic, nostalgic, silly, joyous, poignant, or even bittersweet. I have never been writing from a place of mastery—just one of looking and learning as I go.

Over the last twelve years I have met so many of you. On the blog, in a bookstore, at a conference—even just walking down the street. You know who you are. I know who you are. And I really wanted your heart in this book. So I have woven your letters, submissions, comments, and suggestions into this volume so it hopefully climaxes far from where I started to end somewhere in the great beyond.

My goal is to disappear by the end so that this isn't *my* book of awesome or *a* book of awesome but *our* book of awesome. I hope it serves your home, classroom, community, or, you know, toilet, and I hope it can be a reminder of just how much we have to be grateful for at the end of the day.

And now . . .

A deep pool of awesome awaits us.

So let's strut confidently onto **the pool deck** in our Speedos.

Toss our **sunglasses** on the beach chairs without breaking stride.

And let's look at each other . . . and smile . . . and nod.

And let's start running and jump in.

Neil

Carrying the ice cube tray from the sink to the freezer without spilling

....

You're on a tightrope between towers.

Your long waggly stick is short, plastic, and full of water.

Your wind-bouncing high wire in the sky is the **orange and brown linoleum** between the sink and the fridge.

Crowds line the streets below and you steal a glimpse of wide-eyed children sucking lollipops, an old lady chewing her fingers, and a priest whispering while making silent crosses on his chest.

Pause, close your eyes, take a deep breath.

Stare up to the ceiling and take it step by step by step.

A bit closer, a bit closer, a tip right, a slip left . . . *and you're there!* The crowd roars as you step onto the building ledge, open the freezer door, and carefully set down the tray.

Say goodbye to kitchen puddles, **wet feet**, and lopsided half-filled cubes.

Say hello—or welcome back—to
AWESOME!

Laugh lines

Since skin creases will wedge into cracks and corners through-out our lives, we've only got two real choices on living with them: **love 'em or let 'em bother you**. And if you choose option two, it's a world of fancy creams and face stretching for you.

No, I say get used to them. **Love your wrinkles!** Forehead wrinkles, cheek wrinkles, chin wrinkles: we will have them all. Life will still be a ball and we'll just be telling the world we lived it.

There's something especially beautiful about **laugh-line wrinkles**. I'm talking about the ones in your dimples when you smile, the crow's-feet in the corners of your eyes, and all the little grooves that appear on your chuckling face-scrunching forehead.

Laugh lines are a sign you have lived and lived well.

Congratulations on laughing your whole life.

AWESOME!

Sending a private message during the video conference and then seeing your coworker look down and silently smirk

It's like passing notes in third grade.
AWESOME!

How messy your face is after eating shawarma

....

Pitas aren't waterproof.

Crusty bread sacs are not built for vast swirling ponds of garlic, tahini, hummus, and hot sauce pooling at the bottom of your heavy two-handed shawarma.

You know this. I know this. The guy sawing the **moist crunchy chicken** off the spit knows this. Everybody knows this! So what do we do? Assemble armors of twisted wax and tissue papers, tight aluminum foils, and skinny paper bags so we might briefly delay . . . the gushing.

It happens slowly at first.

A little white drop with an orange oil spot inside it lands on the tray. And just as you notice it . . . there is another. Suddenly you're Malcolm in *Jurassic Park* staring at the plastic cup of water on the dash. Thump, thump, now a drip, now a stream. The wax paper overflow compartments are filling up and you know your shawarma is sinking.

What do you do?

For the love of all that is holy you frantically **bite, bite, and bite** some more. Close your eyes and stab that shawarma like a frenzied shark. Bite that pink pickled turnip, bite that vinegary tabouli, bite those hot crispy fries. Garlic sauce drips down your chin, **hummus mascaras your eyelashes**, and two tiny cubes of chopped tomato briefly clog your nostrils till you lurch back and gasp at the ceiling for air.

Gushing liquids coat your hands and slide down your arms but you keep going and going and going—turning your head sideways for air like you're doing a front crawl—until yes, yes, yes, yes, you are biting bits of wet pita because you successfully made it to the final folds.

Congratulations!

You made it to the end of the shawarma without the whole thing falling into a pathetic wet pile of slop.

Now look up and smile slowly at me as I smile slowly at you. Let's lean back and twirl on our **plastic bolted chairs** and laugh because our faces look like they're coated in cake batter and blood.

Let's stare into the dark, past the glass, past the flashing neon sign, past the barren parking lot, up and over the empty main drag in this quiet town and the dark, dark forests beyond.

It's late, late, late on a Tuesday and everyone is quiet and sleeping but we're out and we're moving and we're wild and we're grooving and we both know this is totally

AWESOME!

Finally unsubscribing from that annoying email you've been getting forever

....

Let freedom ring from the **felt-covered walls** of cubicle farms. Let freedom ring from the dimly lit university dorms. Let freedom ring from phones at the back of the train. Let freedom ring from laptops at the back of the plane. But not only that—let freedom ring from daily coupon deals! Let freedom ring from **annual donation appeals**! Let freedom ring from local sponsorship requests! And let freedom ring from spammy marketing contests!

And when this happens, when we let freedom ring, let's all join hands and sing, "Free at last! Free at last! Look at this empty inbox, we are free at last!"

AWESOME!

Getting really, really sweaty before jumping in the lake

There will be pain.

The moment after jumping off the dock and then splash-landing in an icy body of water is a shocking **Electric Skin Jolt**. But good news! A second later that jolt soothes into a slow-crescendo, full-body **Skin Tingle**.

And that's what we're playing for here: those first few seconds of pins-and-needles pleasure when every part of your skin is getting freeze-kissed at once.

What could possibly amplify the Skin Tingle?

Simply getting really, really sweaty first.

Power-paddling around the dock, hopscotching across scorching sand, diving for volleyballs—all great ways to get really, really sweaty before running off the dock.

Eyes stinging, **back glistening**, it's time to jump into the AWESOME!

Discovering a shortcut the GPS doesn't know about

··

Move over, Marco Polo.

Columbus, Clark, and Cortés, you got nothing, either.

Sure, maybe you sailed over choppy waves and documented life on distant lands. Maybe you traded silk with kings, **discovered precious stones**, and toppled empires.

But we just figured out cutting through the drugstore parking lot saves us ten seconds on the way to the shawarma place.

Beat that.

AWESOME!

Picking the right thing to unplug out of the mysterious power bar full of wires

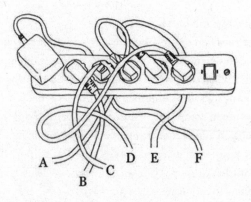

AWESOME!

Completely nailing the timing on that avocado

....

Are you a watermelon knocker?

Sometimes I go to the grocery store and see someone rapping their knuckles on a watermelon. I've talked to a few knockers to understand what they're thinking. Nice deep reverb? Juicy one on their hands. Hollow and flat? Roll that one back into its pen.

Watermelon knockers were my favorite **Fruit Inspectors** until I met an old Jamaican woman plucking leaves from the middle of a pineapple crown. "Tells you if it's ripe," she said to me without looking up. "Comes out easy . . . eat it today."

But what if it doesn't come out easy?

What if you have to tug it really hard?

She looked up at me with tired eyes. "Then eat it tomorrow."

And this is the kind of wisdom I need for avocados.

Bright green, dark green, rock hard, wrinkled and squeezy, we're not lacking things to look for but nothing proves reliable for whether that avocado will be rotten by the time it's sliced open. How terrible is that first sighting of brown splotches, too? You keep slicing to hopefully find **one edible cubic inch of creamy greeny**, but all you get inside are deep black rivery veins. Next it's time to choke back tears and tell your kids you're very sorry but there's just not going to be any guacamole tonight.

A rotten avocado is a sorry situation for everyone.

Farmer sighs and shakes her head, picker lifts his hat and squints into the sun, trucker ugly-cries while nearly veering into oncoming traffic, grocer grimaces and kicks a few pebbles off the black mat at the front of the store.

Nobody wanted it to be this way.

The whole supply chain is disappointed.

And that's why it's such a beautiful moment when you completely nail the timing on that avocado. That's why it's a beautiful moment slicing it open to reveal a perfect bounty inside. Buttery yellow near the pit fading into deep green by the peel. No brown splotches, **no black rivers**, no hard spots, and a perfect score on scoopability.

Every molecule of that avocado's body will be put to use nourishing your body . . . and your soul.

Touch your heart and smile back at the farmer, picker, trucker, and grocer for the perfect job they did delivering the AWESOME!

Accidentally snorting while laughing

....

You just sounded like a pig.
  AWESOME!

Gravy

....

Did you know our Egyptian ancestors first started putting gravy on food over 5,000 years ago? It's true! Hieroglyphics in the tomb of Djer, an early first-dynasty pharaoh, show diners feasting and drinking from gravy boats. Building pyramids is nice, but can we agree that making gravy for the world is even better?

Gravy tastes delicious on Thanksgiving turkey, freshly baked biscuits, mashed potatoes, **french fries**, roasted chicken, country-fried steak, meatloaf from the diner, slow-cooked pot roasts, bangers and mash, pork chops, vegetables, and everything in between.

Breakfast or lunch, **dinner or brunch**, pour it on hams, drench it on yams, straight from the glass, right after mass, gravy, gravy, gravy!

AWESOME!

When your friend returns your book and they actually read it

....

Books are personal sanctuaries of **secret, silent moments**.

Lifting you up, sending you sideways, stirring emotions deep in your soul, reading a book feels like an **invisible adventure**. So when a friend returns your copy and tells you they loved the book, too, it's like they were on the adventure with you.

Let's expand this adventure together right now.

Because we're all here celebrating life's little moments.

Smile and sense us all around you.

As we smile and sense you.

Welcome to *our* book of

AWESOME!

Finding something to scratch the part of your back you can never reach

The middle of your back is no-hands-land.

All those itchy islands off **Spine Beach** see shade and showers, but not much in the way of back-scratching. You can try the **Reverse Angle Elbow-Bender**, but when it fails you'll need to go with one of these classics:

1. **Tree trunks.** Trees! Nature's massage therapists. Yes, in addition to oxygen, shade, and shelter, trees are natural back scratchers. For best results, avoid smooth saplings in favor of the hunched-over, wizened ones full of knots in the middle of the forest. Now covered by most major health plans.

2. **A big metal tool from the barbecue set.** Using the burger lifter or rusty tongs works fine, but for Caveman Bonus Points it's best to go with that one giant fork with the two long, skinny prongs. Close your eyes and you're outside your clifftop cave using a woolly mammoth tusk in front of your blazing fire. Go ahead and pick your teeth with it after.

3. **A golf club from the basement.** Head down the rickety wooden steps and pull the long string hanging from the ceiling. Fish past boxes of rubber wrestling

figures, Fisher-Price telephones, and somehow-still-greasy sandwich presses till you find the big score: Grandpa's old, leathery golf bag. Now it's time to consult your caddy for the best club. Driver? Cumbersome. Putter? Nice but no sharp edges. What's your best shot for this task? Well, Grandpa plunked a lot of shots in the drink. Did he ever ammo up with one of those long, white plastic extendable ball retrievers? If so, that's your best move.

4. **The corner of your wall.** You keep watching football, I'll just casually tiptoe to the corner and rub my lower lumbar all over the pointy wainscoting. Ohhhhh yeah. That's nice. Now I know what the vacuum hose was talking about.

5. **Your cat.** Forget mastering French cuisine, taking years of tennis lessons, or deadlifting yourself into some chiseled hulk. No, I say better to invest thousands of hours mastering the art of getting your kitty to think of your back as a scratching post. Make sure you don't give up after the first few years.

Yes, finding something to scratch the part of your back you can never reach avoids the awkwardness of flipping your T-shirt up, bending over slightly, and asking someone if they'll dig their nails in deep.

Just take care of business yourself and enjoy the skin-tingling rush.

AWESOME!

COMMENTS:

....

Kathy says:

Okay, so I bought a back scratcher at Disney World once. It was awesome, but it broke (too much use?). A friend went to Disney for vacation and I asked him to buy me another one. What did he give me? A Mickey scratcher. What's wrong with it? Mickey's gloved! He does not have sharp nails and so all I get is a soft plasticy mitted scratch which is no scratch at all.

Em says:

Am I the only one in the world who doesn't have a problem with twisting my arms around and scratching my back?

> *Rose replies:*
>
> My guess is you haven't reached middle age yet. Good Luck!

Daph says:

My cat does that every now and then and it's wonderful. BTW, who else suddenly has an itchy back??

Hannah says:

I have an intricately carved silver letter opener lying right in front of me. One pointy end, one flat end. Heaven awaits.

Rogue children

Pancake house beside the highway.

You're chatting in your ripped red polyester booth when a rogue child suddenly appears beside your table. Where did they come from? Nobody knows. You stop to admire this **Junior Runaway** who is clearly living a romantic nomadic life way out past the sticky tables and chairs by the kitchen.

Rogue children are best observed within one to two miles of busy parents. You can find them in furniture showrooms, on crowded beaches, in grocery stores. Keep your eyes peeled for these footloose creatures who are both shy and curious and pose no threat unless threatened, in which case they may bite.

In an age full of flashing screens and endless programming, let's celebrate endangered rogue children whose presence helps reflect back to us the **free-range beauty** and bountiful natural curiosity of childhood.

At the end of the day maybe we're all just rogue children.

Wandering around looking for interesting things.

AWESOME!

Remembering the attachment right before sending the email

Things looked dicey for a minute there but you came through in the clutch.

AWESOME!

Drinking from the hose

It's the buffalo of the backyard.

When you were a kid you lived off that hose. Worshipped friend, mystical enemy, the hose provided ritual cooldowns, endless **sprinkler jumping**, and of course, vital hydration on blazing sun-scorched afternoons.

Some people frown on drinking water from the hose. "It's too hot," they whine. "It tastes like rust." But, what are you going to do when you're already outside, soaking wet? Go inside for a Perrier on the rocks from mom?

No, don't be lame, just pass the snaky drain from under the window pane.

Also, please remember to enjoy hose drinking with the classic **Dribbly Above-the-Head Pour**, the chaotic **Thumb-Stop Surprise Spray**, or even the painful **All-the-Way Power Squeeze** to the back of the throat.

Now can we get back to Tag?

Because you're It.

And you're

AWESOME!

"Shortly after Nate and I started dating, I moved away for school, and then he joined the Navy, and then we were at least 4,141 km apart every day of the year.

Our first Christmas didn't work according to plan. Unfortunately, flights didn't work and the only time we'd have together was in the airport during his two-and-a-half-hour layover. We decided to do Christmas at the airport. We also hadn't seen each other in person for over a year since he left for Naval Training.

I got the idea to give him *The Book of Awesome* and personalize it with comments throughout to make it a really special gift. I spent hours writing in the book. So at the airport, I got Nate to open his present first. He peeled back the paper to reveal the cover and looked at me, shocked, and put the gift down. I told him, 'There's more, open the book!' But he was already reaching in his bag. He handed me a parcel and said, 'Open it.' I looked at him, smiled, and peeled back the paper to reveal the exact same book. We had both created our own personalized books the same way, writing comments all over.

It was a truly awesome airport Christmas."

—*Sarah*

When you finally get rid of that thing that's been rolling around the trunk of your car forever

....

Muted thumps from that half-filled water bottle, **grass-stained golf ball**, or untied pair of skates bang against the side of your trunk and haunt you every turn.

And you think it's annoying and you say you'll get rid of it but when you get where you're going your priorities suddenly shift to getting out, **getting in**, and getting it tomorrow.

That's why it's great when the glorious day finally comes.

When you clean out the trunk and every time you turn it sounds like

. . .

. . .

. . .

—and every time you turn it sounds like

. . .

. . .

. . .

—and every time you turn it sounds like

. . .

. . .

. . .

AWESOME!

When someone calls just to say hi

Conversations can get sharp and edgy wedged into two-point font on tiny screens.

That's why it's so great when your phone actually rings and you actually answer and it's someone calling just to say hi. Whether it's mom checking in before exams, **an old friend you haven't talked to in years**, or your sister across the country just dropping into your day, it always means the same thing.

Someone's thinking about you right now.

AWESOME!

The smell of a library

....

Come on in.

Pull open those **smooth handles** worn to a taffy-colored finish screwed into heavy chestnut doors with big rectangular windows.

As you walk past librarians at waist-high counters, stop to feel the silence spread over everything like a warm blanket.

Massive clothbound atlases, crinkly plastic-wrapped hardcovers, and **sticky picture books** fill rusty metal bookshelves and that thick overly lacquered circular table at the front—dented from that time someone smacked it with their wheelchair years ago.

Did your library have a **Newspaper Room** with glass dining room doors? Did you walk in and see long wooden rods holding the latest issues and three mute, statuesque people reading *The Guardian*, the *Times of India*, or *China Daily*, quietly plugging themselves into a global community?

Every book in the library offers its own **olfactory immersion** as you flip through the pages to that musty sweet spot in the center.

The smell of the library is the smell of sharing stories and tightening bonds between the community we live in today with everyone who came before us.

Hello people of the future.

It's people from the past.

We're all here together right now.

AWESOME!

COMMENTS:

....

An says:

I remember stamped checkout cards . . . I liked seeing the surnames and return dates scrawled on those cards and see if I recognized anyone.

Essa says:

I'm just going to say it . . . it works as a laxative on me!

> *Helena replies:*
>
> So that's why my library's bathroom is always full?!

Marissa says:

In the same vein I love the smell of old churches. The beeswax candles, the incense, the flowers, the musk, all mingling together after years and years of worship.

Jenni says:

I really miss card catalogues. Growing up, I always felt like I was on a mission when I was looking for the right book. Self-checkouts with receipts are lame!

Alicia says:

When I learned how to read there was a book mobile library that drove to my school every week and they had little cardboard library cards and you had to try and trick the librarian into believing you were a preteen so you could take out Babysitter's Club books!

This is my all-time favorite smell. If they could bottle it, I would buy it!

I love the smell of old books, but one smell I love even more is the scent of glossy magazine paper. I'm addicted to it!

I'm a fresh-out-of-school young adult librarian—it's my dream job and everything I wanted it to be. My library smells like bandages (no idea why), and it permeates my hair and clothes. Normally, this would bother me, but since I love my job so much, my workplace is such a great place to be, and the community I work for is so friendly and welcoming, well, the bandage smell is suddenly very appealing.

My childhood library had a bronze fountain of Christopher Robin and Pooh in the middle of the children's section. How peaceful sitting there and reading to the sound of tinkling water. The adult section had two-story-tall stained-glass panels extolling the virtues of reading and learning. They mesmerized me as a girl, and I couldn't wait till I was old enough to get an adult card. It helped me feel like reading was so historic, so formal, so grown-up.

Correctly guessing the secret ingredient

....

Sniffing bean dip, chewing brownies, spooning around curries for clues, you're suddenly a **Flavor Detective** staring at the ceiling while channeling all flavor faculties toward your nose and mouth.

Close your eyes, breathe out slowly through your nose, and swirl that chaw all over your tongue so it touches different taste buds, too.

Doesn't matter if it's something sweet in the cheese dip or **something spicy in the squares**. All that matters is that feeling you get when you know you got it.

Start nodding your head, wink at the chef, and clear your throat loudly so everybody suddenly stops talking and turns to you and sees you reveal a very slow smile before waggling your eyebrows slightly and then opening your mouth to say

"Cardamom?"

AWESOME!

Finishing the workout

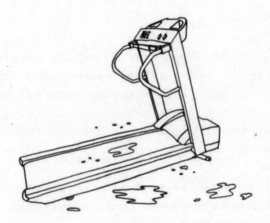

AWESOME!

Hot chocolate in cold arenas

My sister and I took skating lessons when we were kids.

For years my parents piled us into the wood-paneled station wagon and drove us down to the old arena on Sunday nights. Bitter coffee, steamy sweat, and **changeroom mold** hung in the air as we laced up our skates on lacquered honey-colored benches bolted into black foam floors between other three-foot-tall kids in **swishy snow pants**.

I have many fond memories of slamming into the boards, slamming onto the ice, and getting snow shavings into my mitts, but it was always worth it because my parents would buy us **Celebratory Hot Chocolate** at the end of the lessons. I remember skating my last few laps dreaming about that dark sweet liquid splash-spewing into the waxy paper cup from that shuddering brown machine before the old lady behind the wooden counter sprinkled a few small cardboard-like marshmallows on top. She then pushed the burning cup across the counter into my eight-year-old wet, mittened hands without anybody worrying about me possibly tripping over my blades and forever scalding my cherubic features.

Snow melted off our blades and our eyes flashed and sparkled as we wobbled back to those shiny benches holding burning cups . . . flashing beaming smiles.

AWESOME!

Taking the stairs beside somebody taking the escalator

Coming out of the subway, heading to the gates, or strolling back to the office after lunch, you're walking beside someone when you hit that classic fork in the road. On the right is a **smooth-moving escalator** with a bit of traffic and on the left is a **wide-open set of stairs**. As the person beside you steps onto the escalator you jump on the stairs and a starter's pistol goes off.

Jump up those stairs, take them two at a time, do whatever you need to do to beat that **racing bunny** all the way to the top. Celebrate by sucking in huge gasping, wheezy breaths while grabbing your ribs and wiping your shiny forehead on your T-shirt.

Congratulations, friend.

You just burned a calorie.

AWESOME!

Dogs with jobs

....

Dogs are lazy.

There, I said it.

And you know it's true.

Look who's sleeping on the couch, **look who's drooling on my socks**, look who's wandering around in circles. Dogs, my friend, dogs, dogs, dogs.

And sure, maybe **the dog economy** has dried up so it's not as easy to give a dog a bone. But that's why before *this* old man comes rolling home, I suggest we all stop to say thanks to the K9s actually earning their kibble:

- **Seeing Eye dogs.** What was life like for blind people a thousand years ago? Glasses weren't invented yet and we hadn't trained dogs to be backup eyes. Did people like me just walk around aimlessly till we fell into geysers or tried petting hyenas? Well, lucky for us the past thousand years has brought us both glasses from the Italians and Seeing Eye dogs from the French. Seeing Eye dogs deftly avoid geysers, help you get on and off the bus, and look both ways before helping you cross the street, too. Ears perked, always alert, there's a reason we start our list with them. One of the hardest-working dogs in the business.

- **Junkyard dogs.** Who did you think was going to guard all these spare tires, rusty chains, and piles of gravel? Rainstorms, mud puddles, and barbed wire makes junkyard dogging a tough life. But an honest life. A respectable life.
- **Dalmatians on the fire squad.** Apparently, firefighters took Dalmatians with them a hundred years ago because they were a natural barking siren. Their aggressive nature and loud yaps cleared the streets for big red trucks, or, you know, a couple guys holding pails, to race toward the blaze. Dogs of pure heart and courage, these dogs.
- **Bomb-sniffing dogs.** Speaking of courage, do you ever see German Shepherds in the airport sniffing around for duct-taped packages making ticking sounds? That's a job I wouldn't want to do. You neither? Make sure to smile and nod at these noble airport warriors next time you're running in your flip-flops to grab a cinnamon bun before flying home from the beach resort.
- **Sheep dogs.** Herding sheep over grassy hills is no walk in the pasture. While his distant cousins lounge on porches all day before taking a crap on my lawn the far nobler actually-still-herding-sheep sheep dog runs around for hours barking till all those aimlessly wandering sheep all walk the same way. Fierce determination and tireless work ethic are hallmarks of the role.

Dogs with jobs keep the **rusty gears** of our economy creaking as they dedicate their noble lives to service. The least we can do in return is pay them room, board, and a comprehensive benefits plan.

Dogs with jobs, step forward.

Now, step forward. Step! Step!

Siiiiiiiit.

Good dog.

Today we officially declare you

AWESOME!

Adding a gift note to yourself on your online order

....

Dear Angie,

I know you think you don't deserve this and I know
you might even be feeling some guilt or shame at the
idea you even bought yourself this so I want to remind
you that you absolutely DO deserve it and you
absolutely DO NOT need to feel guilty because you
damn well made that money and you damn well earned
that money and who even CARES what Bernard thinks
because Bernard's not in your life anymore and even if
that mo

Error: Over Max Character Limit.

Dear Angie,

You are

AWESOME!

When you find out what was making that horrible smell and get rid of it

My eleventh grade **chemistry class** began with Ms. Serevetas handing each of us a big, broken-spined textbook. A small woman wearing oversized red glasses and a **loose white lab coat**, she introduced herself briskly and began calling us up, one by one, to the front of the room.

It was the first day so we didn't know Ms. Serevetas or many of our classmates yet. Nobody had the guts to start talking or play games. We just stared straight ahead in **mind-numbing silence** while each student shuffled up, collected their ratty textbook, then shuffled back to their desk.

It was a slow and painful ordeal until, out of nowhere . . . one guy's book just suddenly stank.

Something steamy and abrasive filled the room and soon eyes started watering and a few people turned to quietly retch. Poor **Stinky-Book Guy** had no choice but to stare ahead and pretend nothing was happening. "Move along," he seemed to be saying. "Maybe everyone's book smells like farts in a fish market."

But Stinky-Book Guy's stoicism was no match for the building buzz. Ms. Serevetas was forced to take action. She looked suspiciously at Stinky-Book Guy, scrunched her eyebrows, and with a pained grimace began nodding slowly at him. He seemed to get the message and looked down at his textbook to size it up for battle.

And remember: no phones, no screens, just a roomful of teenagers bored out of our minds, so the **Mystery of the Funky Textbook** captivated like fireworks. The room got quiet and everyone craned their necks as he slowly began fanning pages. He started fanning quicker and quicker until a few pages slapped together fast to reveal the location of the stench.

Teeth were clenched, desks grabbed for bracing, and we all watched in horror as Stinky-Book Guy peeled open the pages to reveal an old . . .

rotting . . .

piece . . .

of . . .

salami.

Apparently, someone had the good idea to slide a slice of cured meat between chapters on **Boyle's Law** and **Avagodro's Number** and then leave it steeping in a musty storage closet all summer. Now that once beautifully speckled spicy slice was gray and slimy and had somehow inched itself even closer to death.

There was only one thing left to do and Stinky-Book Guy did it: he bit his lip, nodded forcefully, peeled that salami off, slowly walked to the garbage can, and dropped it in.

The room burst into applause.

One guy cried.

And whether it's the leftover fish in your kitchen garbage, the toilet that wasn't flushed before a long vacation, or the pool of dirty water under the basement carpet, how does it feel to finally find what was making that horrible smell and get rid of it?

AWESOME!

Tire names

....

I went with my first wife to buy tires.

We had never bought tires before so we just listened to the sales guy's advice.

"Eagle Eyes are pretty good," he began, pointing to a stack. "They're better for winter driving than Commanders, but not as good as Snow Claws. But then again, if you're on a budget there's nothing wrong with the Destinys. Sure, they've got lower mileage than the Evertreks or the Never-Ending Trails, but they're going to be better bang for your buck than the Tiger Paws or Peregrines."

Seemingly targeted at the **little sacks of testosterone** hanging in the back of brains, tire names conjure up images of muscles, dirt, and birds of prey. I think we have to presume the big tire companies tested other names but just got thumbs downs from focus groups. I guess that's why you can't buy a set of Flying Chickadees, Sidewalk Skippers, or Puddle Hoppers. Yet, I mean.

A bit of hilarious nonsense we can all enjoy.

Tire names, ladies and gentlemen.

Tire names.

AWESOME!

Opening the dishwasher and it's already empty

You officially live with somebody
 AWESOME!

The sound of the needle hitting the record

....

We didn't used to stream.

After saving money mowing lawns, **shoveling driveways**, or delivering papers, we'd head down to the record shop on Main Street.

Metal bars crisscrossed the door, a rusty newspaper stand holding concert listings was just inside, and as you walked in a tattooed guy standing behind an old counter covered in hundreds of band stickers somehow nodded at you without making eye contact while some **Rolling Stones B side** or jazz album you'd never heard before played in the background.

You walked down the creaky, thin-planked hardwood floors and began flipping through endless plastic-wrapped piles until you found the record you knew you would be taking home that day.

Back in your bedroom you used your teeth to poke a hole in the corner of the tight shrink-wrap, even though your mom always told you not to. Or maybe you used your fingernails to rip a very, very tiny hole in the corner and then expanded that into a very tiny hole and then expanded that into a tiny hole, which then allowed you to stick your finger in and rip it all off. Next you pulled the record out of its sturdy cardboard sleeve and then gently rolled it out of that very thin white paper so that it was finally in your hands—naked, pure, ready.

Did you stop to stare in wonder at how all those tiny grooves could hold all those pianos, drums, and guitars?

After you set it down over the tiny metal nub sticking out of the **rubber turntable mat** you lifted the arm of the record player and carefully set it down on the grooves.

That's when it happened.

The sound of the needle hitting the record is the sound of a magical music moment about to happen. It's the starting pistol before the race, the lightning before the thunder, or the big lion roaring before the movie begins.

It's the sound of waiting, the sound of saving, and the crackly sound of imperfection opening the way . . . into a perfect day.

AWESOME!

Sleeping in sheets that dried in the sun

Drift and dream into that **crispy clean**.

It's always good when you can leave the sheets outside and let the sun do what the sun does best: **heat things up**.

Clothespin your sheets on the line and then just point up at the giant fireball in the sky and say, "Over to you, Inferno!"

Later you'll be spreading those sun-drenched sheets over your mattress and curling into their **warm wind-crumpled arms** as you slide into a cozy world of

AWESOME!

Someone actually returning your wallet

....

Losing your wallet is in *Our Book of Annoying*, that nonexistent netherlist that also includes: when your nacho breaks while picking up the salsa, getting the shopping cart with a wheel that always wants to turn left, and yanking out two inches of floss because the package is suddenly empty and then going ahead and trying to floss with that floss and then not being able to.

Losing a few bills is nothing compared to spending weeks replacing all rectangles of plastic that rule your life. In addition to phone calls with the government and spending a morning down at the DMV, you also have to start that **Buy 9 Shawarmas, Get 1 Free** card again.

And that's also what makes it so sweet when someone actually goes to the trouble of returning your wallet.

Thank you, anonymous stranger!

We hereby declare you

AWESOME!

Peeling all the dried glue off the lid

Finger-picking the crusty, sticky congealed glue off the top of the lid may not sound like fun but it comes off so clean, scratches deep primal instincts, and fills the rest of our day with some smooooooooooth squirting.

AWESOME!

Rejigging the entire 3D puzzle of your freezer to somehow squeeze this giant box of chicken fingers in there

....

3D puzzles should not exist.

All they teach children is masochism.

I was eight years old when some well-intentioned uncle ruined my Christmas. I unwrapped his present and found a 3D puzzle of an apple. How exotic! Clearly word had got out that I was finally ready for the third dimension in puzzling. Prepped to explore terrain few knew about nor ever attempted. For an eight-year-old getting a 3D puzzle for Christmas is like being told you're incredible at climbing rocks so here's a plane ticket for K2.

When I poured the pieces out of the box, I immediately saw the problem. Every piece was tiny, clear, and imperceptibly different from all the others. Round edges, slightly square edges, tiny rectangles out the sides. Nothing seemed to fit together and the photo of a **perfectly 3D apple** on the box provided no assistance. I spent a couple of days working on it and only got three pieces to fit together. I gave up soon after that and hid the puzzle in the back of my closet for years so it wouldn't remind me of my failure.

Well, I am proud to say although it took a few decades, I have finally built my confidence back up. No, I never built that

3D apple, but just look at me turning lasagnas sideways, moving frozen pizzas to the side door, and grabbing a can of lemonade and a tube of croissants for dinner so I can jam this giant box of chicken fingers into the stupid freezer.

Now book me a trip to the mountains, for I am . . . the Puzzle King.

AWESOME!

Grandma hair

....

Grandma hair is any beautifully manicured mane of white hair bundled on top of Grandma's cute and dainty head. It can be hidden under a flower hat, **permed out in cottony waves**, or hung like Christmas tree tinsel in long shimmery strands.

Grandma hair says **I've seen things**. It's a sign of hard-fought wisdom. And it's a sign that Grandma's walked down a long road in life and now she gets to look beautiful at the end of it. If you get old enough to have a **beautifully bright white swirl** of Grandma hair, it's time to say thanks.

Thank you for the life I've had. Thank you for my friends.

Thank you for the memories.

Thank you till the end.

AWESOME!

When that book you placed a hold on four months ago is finally waiting for you at the library

....

Books want to be read.

Focus group a room of hardcovers and you'll hear the same things every time. "Break my back!" a 700-page novel will offer and others will nod. "Underlines and dog-ears are key metrics to building relationship trust," a business book will throw in. "Ohhhhhhhhhh totally agree," a young adult novel will say. "I even like when someone spills coffee on me because it's like a tattoo of a relationship I always want to remember." Everyone nods and takes little sips of ink.

Books want to be read.

Stories spreading through hearts, ideas spreading through minds, help us build bridges across space and time. Almost everything we know comes through books from long ago and our shared history moves through us when we read and pass them along.

When you place a hold at the library, it's fun wondering where that book is right now. Sitting on the dash of a police car, lounging on a **white plastic chair at the pool**, bouncing on the bus in the bottom of a backpack? That book is seeing the world before you meet it, so when you get the notification it's ready, it feels like you're about to go pick up a well-traveled friend at the airport.

Steer your station wagon down to the branch and step inside to find the Holds shelf before scanning for that one crinkle-wrapped hardcover with the rubber band around it with your library card number. And then as you excitedly pick up the book and carry it to the Check-Out desk make sure to ask:

"Where have you been?"

"What have you seen?" and

"Are you ready for another trip?"

AWESOME!

Stretching your legs after a really long car ride

AWESOME!

When the hand sanitizer isn't that extra slippery kind that never dries

....

I love walking into the grocery store.

After I stomp my slushy boots on the black pebble-filled front mat, I put my fists on my hips and pop my chest out in a sweeping gaze over my empire. My armies have sailed the seven seas and brought me mangoes from the Aztecs, cloves from the Indians, cumin from the Kazakhs, **pears from the Mongols**, kiwis from the Maori, arborio from the Venetians, and dates from the Ottomans.

"A ha ha ha ha ha," I bellow deeply, imagining my large round chest pushing against the tight purple silks and gold buttons I am draped in.

"All of this belongs to me!"

And then I see it.

A dirt-smudged hand sanitizer pump hanging by one screw on a **dented pole** six feet in front of my face. A record scratches somewhere in my subconscious and my fantasies of ruling the world blur and disappear.

Now I'm just living in a germy world on a dark and hungry night in the burbs. It's late on a Tuesday and I suddenly just need to get in, **get fish sticks**, and get out.

I squeeze the sanitizer into my hands and pray.

Please don't be that extra slippery kind that never dries.

Please don't be that extra slippery kind that feels like someone on the catwalk at the plant accidentally kicked a can of **industrial-strength lanolin** into the bubbling vat of sanitizer on the factory floor.

We don't want to be stuck walking around the grocery store staring at tall pyramids of green apples and towers of cookie tins just wishing we could touch them without smearing them with slippery grease.

We want the quick-drying stuff that's gone in three seconds and makes us forget about life outside the store so we can briefly get back to the fantasy.

AWESOME!

Feeling your boyfriend or girlfriend smile while kissing you

....

Nothing says love like locking lips.

Whether it's between snoozes on the futon, in the back row at the movies, or swinging from the top of the **Ferris wheel**, it's always a beautiful moment when you close your eyes and connect in a soft and slow embrace.

When you feel the person you're kissing smiling while kissing you, too, it's the **perfect sign** they're enjoying the moment just as much as you.

AWESOME!

Putting all the toppings on the hot dog bun before the actual hot dog

....

What's your local street food?

Pad thai in Bangkok? Gyros in Athens? Hot doughy pretzels flecked with super tiny salt cubes in New York?

I love street food. Most of us do! Local street food calls back our foraging roots, helps cement cultural identities, and lets us all eat what the locals eat . . . the way the locals eat it.

Come visit me in Toronto and we'll grab a street hot dog.

Step under the dirty awning of a tall building on a busy corner and we'll suddenly be standing beside a **shivering old man** flipping hot dogs and sausages on a hot grill under a stained yellow tarp. He'll smile at us and then grab a fork and tiny paring knife to continue cutting little criss-crosses all through the dog so it gets extra crispy.

I've been buying **street meat** since I was a kid and I just love those crispy-on-the-outside-hot-and-salty-on-the-inside hot dogs set perfectly in puffy yellow buns. They make great company for the Blue Jays game or a long walk home late at night after the bars.

Unfortunately, despite the powerful taste Toronto street meat delivers, there is a problem: I'm talking about spillage and plenty of it. Street doggers pride themselves on offering the most toppings possible, so there are endless smudged plastic containers full of relish, chopped onions, dill pickles, grated iceberg lettuce, black olives, green olives, puddly sauerkraut, swimming banana peppers, and lots more rarities including the occasional julienned carrots or Indian pickled mango.

It's all ready and waiting for us to load on right here—under the thin filthy tarp and protected from gas fumes, sewer exhaust, and pigeon crap with nothing more than a few broken plastic lids.

I love the seemingly endless array available, but the physics of balancing piles of wet toppings on round, slippery wieners just doesn't work. I can't tell you how many times ketchup drips have stained my jeans or a **rogue pickle coated in mustard** left a big yellow skid mark right on the belly of my T-shirt. The ladies sure love those.

I kid, but this is a serious problem.

Luckily, there is a solution. Today I am very excited to share **The Toppings-First Method**. Please lean in and listen close, because this just might change your life.

Here's how to pull it off:

Step 1: Ask for your bun while the dog is still grilling. "Mind if I get the bun first?" There, just like that. Most doggers will hand it over. Now you're holding a big empty hot dog bun sitting in a napkin. With me so far?

Step 2: This is the critical bedding step. I cannot overemphasize its importance. You can't just lay wet condiments in the crack of the bun and expect the structural integrity to hold up. That would be ridiculous. No, you need to lay down a layer of bedding first to cradle the wet toppings while preventing them from soaking through. Ideal choices are diced onions, a patchwork of pickles, or lots of grated cheese.

Step 3: With the bedding set you can now confidently pile all the wet toppings on! Deep rivers of ketchup, bright pools of mustard, generous spoonfuls of relish.

Step 4: Dog up! Time to rest that beautiful cooked dog down on your waiting bed of condiments. It might lie high on the bun, but don't worry: everything will still fit. Now your Fat Jim serves as both shield and guide, protecting your pants while escorting the delicious toppings into your hungry belly below.

I learned this magical technique from my friend Chad who takes it to another level by further categorizing all the condiments. Chad can go on long rants about how mustard is necessary to really bring out all the flavors and how even cheese placement is key to fine melting.

My point is that there are more advanced versions of this technique but you need to master the basics first.

Today I have given you a guide.

But only you can do the rest.

AWESOME!

Putting on your sandals and they're all warm from lying in the sun

Slipping on faded flip-flops or cracking Birkenstocks, you get a surprise warm hug and cozy escape from scalding sand.

It's the putting on **warm underwear straight out of the dryer** of summertime.

AWESOME!

When your kids don't hear you opening a bag of potato chips

....

You wouldn't like salt and vinegar anyway, honey.
  I'm eating this whole bag for us both.
  AWESOME!

Inventing new foods at the buffet

Buffets are chemistry labs.

You've got every element on the **Foodiodic Table** sitting in front of you in tiny black plastic containers. Clumps of feta and pickled beets at the salad bar, greasy pizza congealing under table lamps, and mini eclairs sitting pretty in checkered paper wraps.

My favorite buffet was back at my old college dining hall. It was fun eating in a roomful of **scraggly-bearded-and-pajama-pant-wearing teens** buzzing over late Saturday breakfast, getting ready for Friday night, or just hogging out over the lunchtime trough.

Whether your buffet is at the wedding hall, casino, or Chinese restaurant, I'm hoping you always find tipsy piles of heavy ceramic plates and screaming kids scrambling to invent buffet hybrids amid the mayhem.

Let's talk about five of the best:

5. **Curry french fries.** Since big plates of fries are pretty standard at most cafeteria buffets, it's all about figuring out new ways to liven them up. When farty squirts of ketchup and filmy gravy gets old it's time to grab a ladle of curry sauce from the spicy chicken soaking in the metal tin next door.

4. **Apple pie in a waffle cone.** Hey, who says only ice cream gets to enjoy the sugary home of the waffle

cone? Not us! Nope, throw some apple pie in there for good measure or a couple brownies and some whipped cream if you're feeling crazy. Feel free to try the "food in another food's home" technique elsewhere, too. Spaghetti on a hot dog bun, pita pockets filled with meatballs, chicken nuggets on an English muffin, yes, yes, yes.

3. **Chicken finger fried rice.** Most cafeterias are home to bland trays of rice or noodles. And even when you're given some yellow rice with peas or fried rice with tiny cubes of pork, it's still important to upgrade. Chopping chicken fingers into fried rice is a good start. For those with arteries to spare, you can also try to pull off the rare Fried Chicken Fried Rice.

2. **All wonton, no broth soup.** Back when our ancestors were tearing apart buffalo on open plains, I bet there was one jerk in the tribe who would swing by just after the slaughter to swipe a juicy leg. He'd let everyone else peel meat off feet and suck marrow from bones while he sat by the fire chomping on the juiciest piece on the beast. Well, that's kind of what the All Wonton, No Broth Soup Guy is doing to the soup. We don't like them unless they're us. Same goes for Taking-All-The-Shrimp-In-This-Shrimp-Pasta Guy and Stealing-That-Extra-Pepperoni-That's-Technically-On-the-Tip-Of-The-Other-Slice Guy.

1. **Creating a fake version of something you can't find.** No pizza? No problem! Just smear spaghetti sauce on a piece of bread and sprinkle it with cheese from

the salad bar before tossing it in the toaster oven. No tacos? No worries! Fold a pita around some chicken cold cuts and cover it with sliced cheese, shredded lettuce, and barbecue sauce. It's not always pretty, but creating fake versions of something you can't find can help satisfy strong urges.

Inventing foods at buffets is part of who we are.
It's in our blood.
It's in our genes.
It's in our cheap plastic bowls still wet from the dishwasher.
AWESOME!

COMMENTS:

....

Krystal says:

I worked at a buffet and am the proud inventor of the Nugget Sandwich. Take a chicken nugget, top it with a pickle, wrap it in a slice of cheese. You're welcome.

Freddo says:

Hello. My name is Freddo. And I am a Won Ton-a-holic.

Every time I am at a Chinese food buffet, I make myself a little bowl with a handful of nice, juicy Won Tons, and just enough broth to keep 'em moist.

I want to apologize to the guy behind me who just gets to scoop up some salty yellow broth and a few scraggly Won Ton pieces, and maybe a spare scallion or two.

Hopefully I'm just 12 small steps away from change.

Roz replies:

chorus of voices from people sitting in a small circle
    "Hello Freddo."

Connor says:

I was once at this buffet where you could put almost anything on a pancake and I made one with chocolate chips,
white chocolate chips, mini M&M's, pineapples, cherries,
and blueberries. I can still taste it now.

Laura says:

I agree the college dining hall was THE place for this. My
friend Kellen was king of inventions. He'd come back to the
table and we'd stare in wonder at his latest creation. He was
always the guinea pig too—he'd give it a go, and if it got his
approval, we all knew it'd be good. If it was no good then he
was the sacrificial palate.

Freddo replies:

What a useful friend! I definitely need to hang out with
someone who can be my sacrificial palate.. particularly
when I'm worried if the milk has gone sour..

    "Hey Kellen.. come over here and drink this.."
    glug, glug, glug, clump, clump
    Ooops!

"I am an elementary school teacher and it's my job to teach the curriculum, but it is my honor to encourage values, life skills, and positivity in my students. After reading *The Book of Awesome* each student in my fourth grade class recorded their own awesome things for our class bulletin board including: Water balloon fights. Water gun fights. Biting a water balloon. Basketball and wildlife. When you're in the airport or on the plane. Birds singing. Having a nightmare and then waking up to realize it's your birthday. Playing melon tag with root beer. The smell of sunflowers. Playing paintball. Laughing so hard your stomach aches as you roll on the floor and try to breathe."

—Miss Vacrinos & 29 Grade 4 students

When a stranger helps you push your car out of a snowbank

It's the International Community of Snowy Climates.
Thanks for lending a hand.
AWESOME!

Driving down an old road with trees that touch and form a canopy over everything

Sunshine scatters in **speckled shadows** on pebbly roads as you cruise through an old neighborhood on a sunny afternoon. Tufts of grass poke through curb cracks, sewer grates wobble under your tires, and sunbeams gleam off bent basketball rims, brass house numbers, and fire hydrants globby with chipping paint.

And above it all tall trees on both sides of the street are punching their **skinny crooked fists to heaven** and spreading leathery leafy arms up and over the world.

Feel their energy as you roll slowly through the polka-dotted tunnel.

Breezes whisper . . .

Sparrows sing . . .

As your heart flutters and flips into the AWESOME!

Yellow teeth

....

Teeth were not meant to be neon.

The way it's become with the strips, gels, toothpastes, baking soda this, dental bleaching that, it almost seems like **Having Ridiculously Bright White Teeth** is quickly becoming another mandatory personal hygiene norm—landing in the tin with a hollow clank beside showering every day, cutting our hair, and wearing deodorant.

Well, to this madness I say: **Stop!**

Can we just settle down and calmly rethink this whole situation before it gets out of hand? Can we have a group discussion—right here, right now—about collectively rejecting unnaturally bright white teeth and going back to the way things were?

Yes, I am indeed talking about the yellow teeth of our youth, the au naturel teeth, the teeth you grew up with, the modest *aw shucks* pearly yellows of Joe Everyman and Jane Everylady. Let us embrace teeth that get stained with coffee and smoke and tomato sauce and Indian food. Red wine! Dark roasts! Turmeric-laced curries! Bring it on.

We need to welcome back the teeth that love us no matter who we are or what we eat.

And can I add: research shows white teeth hurt. We're talking hot and cold sensitivity, weakened enamel, and receding gum lines. Not pretty. Don't get addicted to the whitening stuff. No, we like having you around. Nobody wants to find you **sprawled face-down** on a stained motel room carpet, a dozen squeezed-out packs of Crest Whitestrips lying beside you on the floor.

So come with me, come back to the world where teeth are yellow, just the way they were meant to be. And next time a little kid comes up to you, points you square in the mouth and says, "Hey, buddy! Your teeth are yellow!" just lean on your fence post and say, "Why, yes . . . Yes they are, little slugger. And you know? I think that's allllllllllllllllllllrrriiiiiiiiiight."

AWESOME!

COMMENTS:

....

Farrell says:

Yellow teeth are a natural sign of aging, like laugh lines, gray hairs, crow's-feet, wrinkly elbows, cellulite, etc. Our over-marketed, consumer-driven, skinny-model-obsessive society needs to remember this and fight back against all the advertising trying to tell us otherwise! This page is a good reminder we are awesome even though, or maybe because, we are flawed!

Eileen says:

I'm a dental hygienist and imperfect teeth add character. I much prefer natural color and alignment over perfectly-straightened-and-overly-whitened teeth.

Don says:

I have a chip in one of my crooked, front teeth. Sometimes, I think it's pretty awesome.

Jenny replies:

I have straight teeth from braces but one of my front teeth got chipped afterwards. It's also ended up a bit shorter than the other one. I love it, I'd never get it fixed.

Walter says:

I had a chronic condition as a child that caused me to throw up frequently. This resulted in yellow teeth. I've always been extremely self-conscious about my teeth to the point where I didn't even want to read this page after I saw the title. But now I feel better and I am smiling proud today!

Erin says:

APPLAUSE Today is the day I really try to stop feeling self-conscious about my yellow teeth!

Daniel says:

I can't stand the sight of yellow teeth and I'm not a shallow person. I think everyone here is disgusting.

Putting a couple easy things on your to-do list just so you can enjoy crossing them off

....

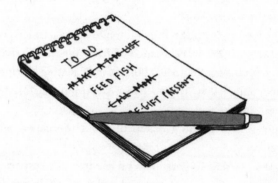

AWESOME!

Reading an actual newspaper

We used to read newspapers.

Do you remember waking up on Saturday or Sunday morning and tiptoeing onto the cold porch to grab that tightly wound paper in the plastic bag?

After tossing it on the kitchen table, you'd tear it open and fill the air with the warm stench of fresh ink, plastic bag, and morning dew. Next you peeled off that **disgusting black rubber band** and unrolled it till you had a bumpy beautiful stack of crisp fresh news.

There was something beautiful about the paper before it was opened.

Strawberry jam fingers hadn't dog-eared any corners, flyers weren't scattered everywhere, and awkward **backward-folding** hadn't flipped sections inside out, making them flimsy and disorganized—untethered middle sheets slipping onto the orange and brown linoleum.

It was a window to the world from your kitchen table.

When you flipped open the paper, there were kids huddling under cars in distant countries, stern-eyebrowed generals swearing in to lead violent armies, and tornados blasting barns to bits, all photographed inches away, **just yesterday**, sitting in your hands right now.

And there were no distractions, either.

Alerts didn't pop up, texts weren't a click away, and detergent jingles didn't scream out of random corners. Everything faded into the **Backyard Background** as you got sucked into tales of police corruption, stunned by fiery photos, or captivated by a two-page profile of the local high school athlete on a comeback bid.

While reading the paper your fingers slowly turned black with **ink smudges** that stained your body like tattoos. The newspaper . . . marked you. While you were leaving greasy prints in its cracks and corners, it was leaving something with you. In a way you touched each other, **traded molecules**, and slowly became one.

Columnists felt closer to real people back then, too, like someone you could actually run into at the grocery store. There was the sharp-tongued sports writer who hated ownership but loved the game, the **provocative political pundit** with the bleeding heart, and the snobby movie critic whose biting reviews kept you laughing for days.

Crystal clear voices and friendly faces in tiny boxes felt like chatting with friends. You even missed them when they went on vacation and all you got was the heart-sagging line on F3: "Dave Perkins will be back next week."

That was when the game was more of a story than a score, when ideas came in paragraphs instead of bullet points, where the vast artistic breadth and complexity of a three-hour epic wasn't squeezed into a simple two-digit percentage.

Newspapers offered connection and community, too.

It was less **The Newspaper** and more **Our Newspaper**.

A poem caught your eye in an obituary, a snarky letter to the editor got you laughing, and crossword puzzles kept you and Gramps guessing all day . . . since there was no real way to figure out the answers till tomorrow. Flipping through the paper was an escape from your head. A half-hour vacation into faraway worlds where you were suddenly attending film festivals, trying **banana walnut bread** recipes, and test-driving a new car . . . all from your front porch. Garage sale ads, furniture for sale, want ads for Main Street shops, and missed connections all popped up and mixed together like a **community cacophony** that felt like the whole town was on a big group text. You could almost put your ear to the pages and hear accents, voices, and histories of the paper's community slowly swirling together into one.

Newspapers acted as filters against overwhelm and misinformation. Was there less choice? Harder to find diverse opinions? Sure, yeah, of course. But overhead limited spam, space limited excess, and deadlines prevented minute-by-minute all day updates from **buzzing phones**.

When there was an end-of-season sale at the ski shop, they splurged for a full-page ad. When a new school was proposed downtown, they advertised a meeting in the high school gym. When your neighbor's daughter finished college, there she was in her black graduation cap, frizzy hair poking out like a triangle, a beautiful all-braces smile, in fuzzy black and white.

Long, long time ago, I can still remember . . . how that paper used to make me smile.

Now fat weekend papers have gotten thinner, foreign bureaus have gotten dimmer, and there's bad news on the doorstep . . . with algorithms replacing local depth.

Sure, time changes, **life changes**, the world spins and moves on. Maybe we're all fitter, happier, and more productive, and maybe we have more choices, **greater access**, and increased transparency. But that doesn't mean we can't enjoy those papers from our past, too.

Next time you walk past an old paper stand, snap a dirty rubber band, or fold tall thin sheets back in your hand, make sure you enjoy the feeling, the moment, and the memories.

Remember the joy of reading an actual newspaper.

Remember to remember it's
AWESOME!

Unpacking the last box

....

Packed boxes are ghosts.

After you move into your **shiny new place** those cardboard demons haunt your hallways and basements for months. You see them hiding behind drain pipes in the storage room, **lingering between boots in the closet**, and even subbing in for pieces of missing furniture. Shoutout to anyone else who's had a corrugated bedside table.

But that's why it's deeply satisfying when you finally unpack the last box. Stash the gravy boat in the dining room cupboard, throw the photo albums on the shelf, and drop the baby clothes in the donation bin.

You just exorcised your demons of laziness.

AWESOME!

Throwing non-ball objects to people

Why walk?

Tossing something from a distance saves you an annoying **six-second commute** around the kitchen counter and since we evolved the ability to suddenly hear someone scream before turning to see something flying right at our face, it's good practice to keep the skills fresh. Just remember to start with the basics and move your way up the chain.

Level 1: Apples and oranges. Fruit is a low-risk starting point. Drop an orange? No big deal. And that rolling grapefruit is just as juicy and delicious as before. Spongy brown dent in your apple? Completely edible. Now, I will say getting beaned with a banana stem could leave a mark, but that just means next time you're hanging with the guys down at the roller-skating rink you can earn some toughness points by just pointing at your shredded forehead and nodding slowly.

Level 2: Keys. There's a lot to grab onto here so this is still the minor leagues of throwing and catching non-ball objects. Fingers stabbing through rings, jingly keys catching on wild fingers, no problem, piece of cake. Just be sure you don't underestimate the surprise aerodynamics of a mini-flashlight, garage door opener, or squishy-ball key chain. No shame in using two hands.

Level 3: Phones. Phones are the perfect size and weight for throwing but they include the side risk of shattering the screen into a thousand pieces. I recommend starting in front of cushion-covered couches and working up to across-the-busy-highway when you're ready. No need to rush it.

Level 4: Unopened cans of soda / bottles of beer. Pulling out an ice-cold can of soda from the bottom of the melted freezing water in the backyard baby-blue cooler is a great start. Whipping it across the deck to your thirsty friend is a great finish. There is some explosion risk, but when you're in the big leagues you're in the big leagues. Time to sidearm a glass bottle of root beer across the deck or go home. If you're not ready, go back to clementines.

Level 5: Raw eggs and water balloons. Company picnics, family reunions, and summer camps are the height of tossing non-ball objects to people. But if you climbed the other four levels before getting here, I'm pretty sure you won't be the one covered in salmonella. No need to thank me. Remember: you got here yourself.

Now, if you master level 5, you're ready for the Masters program, which includes The Over-The-Campfire Beer Grab, Front-To-Back-Of-The-Van Hamburger Toss, and Reverse-Angle Cat Snag.

Tossing non-ball objects to people is such a great high.

A brief second of air-sailing fun in the middle of your day.

AWESOME!

Finding and eating berries right off the vine and they're all warm and juicy from the sun and then the juice dribbles down your chin

....

Primal shrieks of delight from distant nomadic ancestors resonate deeply through your soul.

AWESOME!

Sitting on that warm spot where your pet was just sleeping

Mmmmmmm.

When you're looking for a good snooze in warm sheets or a cozy chill session on the couch, it's wonderful landing in that warm spot where the dog or cat was just snoozing.

Especially on a chilly day.

AWESOME!

"After I was diagnosed with cancer my girlfriend Theresa gave me *The Book of Awesome* as part of a 'feel good' gift. Not only do I enjoy re-living the AWESOME moments I've also enjoyed living some new personal AWESOME moments since my diagnosis: (1) listening to my 3.5-year-old daughter laugh hysterically as she pats my bald head, (2) watching my 3-month-old son go from confused to happy when he figures out who I am (poor little guy can see me in a wig/scarf/hat/bald all within a short time frame), (3) continuously getting blown away by acts of kindness, generosity, and thoughtfulness from friends and family. Thank you to EVERYONE who has done something AWESOME for a friend today!"

—*Brigitte*

Any dessert in sandwich form

Let's do this.

It's time to break down the top six.

6. **The Creamy Zebra.** The classic soft rectangle ice cream sandwich melded into the wall of sinusoidal ice shavings near the bottom of your corner store freezer. Push your paws between Popsicles and pre-wraps to grab the sticky surprise from the frozen tundra. Next, drop a couple dollars on the counter before slowly undressing the Wax Paper Tuxedo to reveal your naked bounty: jet-black dimpled cookies melted right onto a factory-chopped rectangle of vanilla ice cream that offers one entirely soft consistency with zero texture variation.

5. **Illegally Sized Oreos.** Painstakingly twist apart as many Oreos as you can, slow-peel the sugary icing off of each one, and then rebuild it into a majestic Oreo full of as much of the white stuff as possible for the ultimate sugar to cookie ratio.

4. **The Donut.** This is where a freshly fried glazed donut has been sawed in half and stuffed with ice cream, maybe some chocolate, maybe some cinnamon sugar. Yes, it's an endangered species, but with recent carnival conservation efforts, the donut sandwich is

making a comeback. My friend Gillian recently told me about one she ate at a local fair: "It was the hottest, freshest donut," she began, "and the coldest, creamiest vanilla ice cream." Her eyes glistened like a honey cruller as she gazed off into the distance. I could tell the donut affected her, moved her in some small way.

3. **The Wild Zebra.** This is where you pull off the same black-and-white ice cream sandwich as Creamy Zebra, except it's made to order at your own house. You buy crunchy cookies. You scoop fresh ice cream. You put them together. It's all you! None of this store-bought garbage. It's the difference between seeing a zebra in the zoo and seeing a zebra on the African plains. The zebras may look the same but they taste completely different. That's not what I mean. Not *tastes* like you're eating zebras from the zoo and you're also like a zebra poacher who shoots and eats zebras in the Serengeti and, you know, those poached wild zebras with real developed running muscles and big swooshing tails, yum yum, they taste way better than lazy, diseased, fat old zebras from the zoo who sit around in the wrong climate for twenty years eating hay bales and candy wrappers. I'm not saying that! I didn't shoot any zebras. Nor did you! Nor should you, I mean. I don't know anything about zebras. What I do know is you should make your own ice cream sandwiches in your own backyard and then never lazily compare them to something they do not

resemble in any way at all other than they happen to have the same colors. Clearly.

2. **Cake Sandwich.** There's a burger stand near my house that's only open in the summer due to their lack of roof. But, when they are open it's a special place because they have rows of picnic tables, bean bag tosses, and a big bonfire in the center with a delicious smoky smell. The servers run around holding burgers, dogs, and fries and when you're done they always say: "Would you like an ice cream sandwich?" And you say, yes, of course, because hashtag yolo. Then they say, "Do you want chocolate chocolate, chocolate vanilla, or vanilla vanilla?" And you pick one without fully getting that they're about to bring you a giant rectangle of (chocolate or vanilla) frozen birthday cake, sliced across the gut, with a perfect rectangle of (chocolate or vanilla) ice cream gently placed inside like some sort of frozen child tucked into a puffy, sugary duvet. Everyone's eyes pop when the masterpiece is set down on the checkered tablecloth and then afterwards the bean bag toss goes into a sort of riled and frenzied triple overtime just due to blood glucose levels.

1. **The Crazy.** This is the one you make at three in the morning in the giggle-till-you-pee-your-pajamas stage of the sleepover. Somebody gets a craving after the movie, but the pizza boxes are just full of rock-hard crusts and limp green peppers, so while your parents sleep upstairs you all slip out of your

sleeping bags, pound up the basement steps, flick on the kitchen lights, and pull the waffle iron out of the pantry. Batter splatters, giggles amplify, and a **couple burnt forearms** later you're peeling waffle after waffle from the machine. But it doesn't stop there! Someone sizzles up bacon, maple syrup glug-glugs, and your host finds a leftover stash of Halloween candy. An hour later you're back into sleeping bags with all your friends leaning around one plate tearing apart a sloppy sandwich full of ice cream, bacon, shaved coconut, and gummy bears. It's a primal savanna kill short on majesty but long on memories.

Now!

These are just a few dessert sandwich possibilities.

We have come so far but the future is bright, my friends.

One day we will achieve the **Dessert Sandwich Singularity** where all combinations merge together seamlessly and we can't even remember which desserts were ever eaten separately.

Do not be afraid of this progress.

Do not be worried.

While there may be job losses at the ice cream parlor or The Cheesecake Factory, the truth is our economy is robust and entirely new roles and organizations will be created such as the ice-cream-and-Korean-tacos parlor and The Cheesecake Cold Cut Factory.

The future will be magnificent. The future will be glorious.

And the future will be truly

AWESOME!

Deciding to ignore that little pain you woke up with today and hoping it will just go away tomorrow with a good night's sleep

....

And then it does.
    AWESOME!

A little kid holding the door for you

AWESOME!

When a human answers the phone

Are you sick of calling computers?

It's a frustrating ordeal. I'm always like, "Option Seven, please. No! Se-VEN! Seven. Seven! No, back. Go back. Previous Menu. **MENU! MENU! MENU! BACK!**" and then I get so frustrated I end up hanging up but then, of course, I end up calling right back because I still need that thing I was calling about the first time, but this time when I call back I really do try to listen but the menu is just so long and slow that at some point I zone out and stop listening carefully but then I catch myself not listening carefully so I suddenly start listening carefully again just praying the final option will actually be the chance to talk to a real person and so when I finally hit the phone bot saying, "And Press 0 to hear to all these options again," I feel like throwing my phone at the wall but I don't because I *still* still need to figure out my thing and yet I know I can't handle calling back a third time so I try frantically pressing 9 or 8 or 7 in the hopes of triggering a phone ringing on a real person's desk or I sometimes just start screaming directions to trigger something like "Request agent. AGENT! Aaaaa-gennnnnt. MENU! Main menu, main menu? AGENT!!!" Sometimes when I do this I accidentally click the option that leads to the incredibly slow 45-second mailing address readout and that's precisely when that **thick blue vein** in my forehead starts throbbing.

See, that's why it's great when a human answers the phone.

We're not always great talkers, me and you. We don't speak binary, we have strange questions, we don't always know what we need. Option 3 might not explain what kind of credit we get if we cancel our flight and Option 6 can't answer the question about what this weird charge is on our bill.

We need a fellow human to get things moving and we need a fellow human to help us out.

Today let's stop to give high fives and big cheers to companies that ditch electronic prisons in favor of sending us to someone who actually helps.

AWESOME!

When you cook something new and everyone likes it

I can still remember the taste.

First date went well, second date went well, so I invited her to my apartment for a home-cooked meal on the third. I was a year out of my divorce and my standard dinner was a plate of nachos and **a spoon of Nutella** for dessert, so I knew I needed to up my game for the big night. "This could be the first date we tell our grandchildren about," I thought to myself.

Safe to say I had high hopes.

And everything started well.

I'd found a fancy pasta recipe online and raced through the grocery store after work loading up on ingredients I had never bought before: sun-dried tomatoes soaking in thick yellow oil, **artichoke hearts squeezed into tiny square jars**, and a bottle of dry white cooking wine.

Then I came home and made a big mess.

First, I somehow didn't have butter, so I tossed the chopped onions into some **lukewarm olive oil**. Then after I realized I forgot to buy garlic I dumped the whole bottle of artichokes in to make up for it—assuming they were related somewhere back in the **Vegetable Family Tree**. My date arrived as I was frying the onions and I quickly pulled out a chair for her while rushing back to the stove to notice the artichokes all dissolving to mush.

With my grip on dinner suddenly slipping, I tried to valiantly **save the day** by pouring half a bottle of white wine into the pot and letting the whole thing simmer for ten minutes.

I breathed a sigh of relief, washed my hands, and scooped a bed of **steaming pasta** onto a couple dinner plates before ladling a generous amount of sauce on top.

I can still remember the taste.

The onions were somehow **raw and burnt** at the same time, the artichokes had long melted to fumes, and the booze hadn't simmered off so the entire meal tasted like **hot wine**.

It was a horrible eating experience and we choked it back through **forced smiles** and hot tears. A shaker of parmesan and a pepper grinder were called in to help, but they were just pounding the chest of a lifeless corpse.

She went home soon afterwards.

After I helped her put on her coat she turned and gave me a sad smile and a courtesy hug.

I never saw her again.

It was a sad night but it made me want to experience the joy of cooking something new and everyone liking it.

I can see it now . . .

see it now . . .

see it now . . .

After flipping through glossy cookbooks I whip through the gourmet grocer before carrying two perfectly packed brown paper bags through the marble lobby of my sexy downtown apartment. Then I tie on a full-body apron, **pull my flowing hair into a bun**, and dramatically step onto my lush penthouse garden deck to light my titanium smoker. Cue music montage of me grating squeaky green cabbage for coleslaw, slow-frying pancetta for potato salad, and peeling a bunch of sticky overripe bananas.

And then my well-dressed party walks in and suddenly heels tap wooden decks while glasses clink and a sweet smoky smell starts filling the room.

I don't break a sweat as I serve the meal.

And then the compliments begin.

"Ohhhh . . ." someone says softly, biting into sticky meat that falls off the bone on the first bite. "This is delicious! What's in the sauce?"

But I never tell them.

Because I like the attention.

I just smile and listen to their praise.

"Fresh corn bread? I'll take a corner piece!"

"Capers in the salad? A delightful surprise!"

"Warm banana cream pie? You didn't!"

"We all think you are just incredibly
AWESOME!

Leaving your belt in your pants for tomorrow

Congratulations, Superdresser.

You just shaved twenty seconds of **winding a belt** through six denim loops while rushing to get to work in the morning.

Also applies to leaving shoelaces tied up, **keeping T-shirts inside hoodies**, and sleeping with your glasses on.

AWESOME!

COMMENTS:

Kristina says:

I've been sleeping with my watch on ever since I got a watch. I never realized what a time saver it was until this page. I suddenly appreciate the extra five seconds of sleep I've been taking for granted for the last 18 years!

Freddo says:

I sometimes leave my jeans looking like they were just dropped to the ground straight from my body and stepped out of and then step back into the leg holes and pull up my jeans the next morning!

Jdurley replies:

Have you ever visited the fire station, Freddo? They have, like, whole outfits staged so they can just jump in, boots and all. We can all learn from the firefighters.

Lara says:

And you can save even more time by skipping the belt (who has time to deal with buckling it?) and investing in a good strapless bra so you don't even have to take off the shirt you slept in.

Connor says:

I haven't untied my shoes in at least a month. Ten seconds can make the difference between making and missing the bus!

When the internet goes down and everybody walks out of their rooms and actually starts talking to each other

....

"Is your internet down?"
  "Yeah, yours?"
  "Yeah."
  . . .
  . . .
  . . .
  . . .
  . . .
  . . .
  . . .
  "So how long you been living above the kitchen?"
  AWESOME!

Making disgusting slurping noises while eating a really juicy peach

Dive in teeth-first and feel that ripe peach flesh flashflood your mouth with its sweet and juicy waterfall. Orange drips start streaming onto your fingers so fast you might have to switch to the **Flying Saucer Landing** move which involves tilting your head straight back and eating the peach above your mouth for controlled drippage.

Rogue peach juice splashing your eyes keeps coming so when you're past the first few bites it's time for the classic **Sucker Fish Liplock**, where you completely cover the stringy open wound of your peach and suck as much juice out as you can.

Next, go for the **Dry Bone Break Off**, where you pull off the last few chunks of peach flesh without leaving a single peach molecule sticking to the pocky brown pit.

Grunts, squeals, and vacuum cleaner noises are all completely acceptable.

Slurp for the moment,

Slurp for the memories,

And slurp . . .

. . . for your life.

AWESOME!

3:00 a.m. driveway conversations with your best friend

....

I grew up in the burbs.

Streetlights scattered **buttery yellow glows** on empty streets and dark houses. Going out late meant entering small worlds in bedrooms and basements far away from the dimly lit parks outside.

Whenever those hangouts finished, the scene always cut quickly to **late night car cruises** through warm summer breezes till everyone was dropped off at driveways ten blocks away.

And if you were the last to get dropped off you might occasionally score a beautiful 3:00 a.m. driveway conversation with your best friend.

Curfews were cute but getting home late meant nothing compared to the magical connections you always got when there was nowhere else to go.

"I worry about . . ."

"I wonder if . . ."

"I'm scared to say . . ."

"I think about . . ."

"I haven't told . . ."

"I'm waiting for the day . . ."

Deep thoughts, **dark thoughts**, head twists and turns—there's just so much to burn when the moon's up, the sun's down, and you're alone with a loving friend.

AWESOME!

Taking the price tag off anything in one clean peel

Have you ever waged a quiet, ten-minute war against a stubborn price tag?

Slapped on the side of a souvenir, stuck to the bottom of a vase, you start peeling it off with your fingers. But then it happens—a quick tear and you're holding a **sad little scrap** in your hand.

That's when it's time to roll up your sleeves and pull out the edge of the credit card or twist open a bottle of nail polish remover and start pouring it on. Nothing is off-limits as you fight for your right to give a non-sticky action figure to your nephew on his birthday.

You rub in oils and lotions, scratch your fingernails in there, and finally, **huffing and puffing**, you smear it all off with an occasional sticky shadow of the price tag remaining.

This is why it's important to just smile and love it lots when that tag rolls off in one smooth peel.

AWESOME!

COMMENTS:

....

Missy says:

Some newer price tag stickers are made to come off with little effort but they are nowhere near as satisfying as scraping off old ones which I can only assume were attached with thin layers of cement.

Meg says:

How about those tags that have the little circles to prevent the swappage of prices? Extra special if you get one of those off without leaving any circles behind.

Sylvie says:

Don't forget the joy of having the sticker roll up taquito style once you finally manage to peel it off . . .

    Mel replies:

    Taquito style! Also great when you think you're defeated because the tag starts ripping, but you start again on the other side and voila! It's a one-piece paradise.

Tessa says:

When I was fourteen my school actually had a price tag peeling CONTEST!! And the best part was I won by peeling 32 price tags PERFECTLY!!

That secretary who actually runs things around here

She's mind-spinningly fast when it comes to simple tasks that trip others up like double-sided photocopying while filling the legal-sized paper tray at the same time. He seems to have a sixth sense at all times for figuring out which of these tiny keys belong to this stupid locked filing cabinet.

That secretary who actually runs things around here keeps the **top brass** organized so well that it usually becomes a joke with lines like: "We'd be lost without Jo!" "Sunjeev runs this place!" Or "If Barb goes on vacation, it would be chaos!"

These lines are usually funny until Barb does go on vacation. **And it is chaos.** Now the lunch meeting has no lunch, there's no computer for the boardroom presentation, and accounting hasn't got anybody's expense reports on time because a wildly growing haystack of crinkly receipts is just sitting on Barb's desk.

Today we stop to say thanks to that secretary who actually runs things around here.

You make our schools, **offices**, and indeed our lives AWESOME!

COMMENTS:

....

Linseed says:

Secretary? Secretary? Secretary? What's that????? I haven't heard that one in about 30 years. How about this one: administrative assistant. AND—get this: "She" isn't always a "she"—the best "secretary" I ever had was my executive assistant—a "he." How about this: The PERSON that actually runs things around here.

> *Erin replies:*

> I don't mind being called a secretary one bit. It's who I am. It's what I do. I've always thought that someone who insists upon being called an 'administrative assistant' sounds like someone who feels like the title of 'secretary' is beneath them. If it's what you do, own it, and be the best one there is!

Beck says:

I was once one of said Secretaries, and things did literally fall apart when I would go away on holidays! I would have to do the equivalent work before going away just to make sure it wouldn't die without me there. At my company we called these Secretaries "The Boss" as they know more about how things work than the actual boss.

> *Gina replies:*

> "Do you want to speak to the man in charge or the woman who knows what's going on?" That sign was actually posted in my high school office.

Annie says:

We had one of those secretaries in my elementary school and she was so popular she had her own parking spot and on her birthday we had an assembly to celebrate her!!! She knew every student's name, their family, and could fix any situation!!!

Sébastien says:

Too bad they rarely have the wage they deserve . . .

> *Claudia replies:*
>
> Bien dit, Sébastien!

Michelle says:

This is me! Thank you to all of you on behalf of those of us who are largely overworked, underpaid, and underappreciated (except by my CEO, who loves and adores me and buys me chocolate and alcohol).

Chrissy says:

My grandmother had to return to work in her later years after my grandfather suddenly died. She ended up becoming a receptionist at a community college and for years took on "extra tasks as assigned." When she retired they hired three people to replace her—no one could figure out how she'd been getting through all her work in addition to running the huge, 1980s switchboard.

Finding a lid that fits this stupid Tupperware container on the first try

Problems start with the fact that every Tupperware has two pieces. There is a container. There is a lid. Some lids fit on two containers. Other lids look like they do. And nothing ever seems to add up.

You would think there would be more lids than containers in the cupboard since **solo containers** are more likely to disappear holding sliced grapes for the kids on a car ride or get left full of **burnt popcorn kernels** beside the basement couch. But somehow that never happens. Instead, lids disappear into the abyss and you're left standing in the kitchen in high heels at eight in the morning—lidless, lonely, late for work—awkwardly switching dishes and screaming until you finally end up carrying your samosa in a cake container.

That's why it's great when you find the right Tupperware lid on the first try. You breathe a big sigh of relief realizing you just saved a **frantic five minutes** on your hands and knees digging through plastic scrap heaps on a cold tile floor.

Taking leftovers to work in peace?

AWESOME!

The core of the cinnamon roll

It's the center of all taste.

The icing has **crisped just slightly** so your teeth sort of puncture it into tiny sugary shards, revealing the softer, more liquidy layer below. All the drier outsides of the cinnamon roll are long bitten off so you're holding something more doughy, fragile, and floppy. There is usually more cinnamon here, too, and if you're lucky it is dark, speckled, and molten. The core of the cinnamon roll is also the tallest part of the roll, which means you've got a much larger variety of textures to choose from. Will you bite off the sticky sweet top, slowly twist apart the **fresh-bready innards**, or squish the whole thing into a tiny cube of dense and concentrated cinnamon sweetness?

Decisions, decisions.

AWESOME!

When the crosswalk changes to walk just as you approach it

It's like the universe knew you were coming.
AWESOME!

Tiny sports victories

I'm terrible at sports.

Yes, when I was a kid I retired from soccer after just one season. In my final game I took a booted ball right to the face which **snapped my glasses** in two and caused me to crash to the field in a wet, slobbery mess. Unfortunately, since we were low on players and couldn't forfeit the big playoff game, I was forced to hang out in the corner of the field, blind and drippy, until the whistle blew.

Anyway, it wasn't just soccer. I hung up the cleats after one season of baseball, too. Somewhat improbably I managed to both bat fourteenth in the lineup and lead my team in **hit-by-pitches**. This was less because I crowded the plate with gritted teeth and steely determination and more because most twelve-year-olds can't throw straight and I have very slow reflexes.

Since I'm awful at sports, I tend to over-celebrate any type of tiny sports victories I get. To be clear: I'm not talking about shooting any buzzer-beating three-pointers or catching a winning touchdown in the corner of the end zone, no. I'm talking about any **teeny-weeny play** during the game where I actually get to feel like I did something right for a second.

Let's talk about five favorites:

5. **The Air Hockey Self Score.** This is where your opponent fires the round plastic puck so hard it caroms

off your end and slips into the little slit on their side. You scored by being unable to do absolutely anything. Well done! Cap your celebration by cupping your ear with your hand and pretending the deep hum from the hundreds of air holes is the crowd cheering from the upper deck.

4. **The Accidental Pool Shot.** Here's where you aim for the six ball near the corner pocket but miss completely and send the cue ball spinning wildly around the table until it accidentally bumps another ball into a completely different pocket. We'll take it!

3. **Rim Rollers.** Okay, moving to basketball: A rim roller is when your shot bounces off the top of the backboard and clangs around for ten seconds, bouncing off the rim three times, before eventually, reluctantly, slow-spinning around the rim and falling into the basket.

2. **The Slow Strike.** If you're as bad at bowling as me, then you love that moment once every ten games when your ball barely nudges a corner pin and causes a bizarre slow-motion domino effect that fifteen seconds later adds up to a strike.

1. **The Tennis Drop-off.** Here's my favorite of all. When you win a point in tennis by hitting the ball into the tape at the top of the net and it immediately falls over and dies on the other side, that's just perfect.

Now I know what you're thinking: These are all **cringeworthy cheap shots** no athlete would be proud to score. But I'm no athlete, people. I'll take my tiny sports victories when I get 'em if I get 'em.

And I'm not too proud to admit it, either.

Who's with me?

AWESOME!

COMMENTS:

Chad says:

The only time I get a 300-yard drive in golf is when I bounce it off the cart path.

Ian says:

A footy-related one: When you inadvertently bump the ball off your standing foot and it helps you get past a defender and look skillful in the bargain.

> *Gord replies:*
>
> My best accidentally awesome soccer story: chasing the ball beside a player from the other team, tripped, fell, did a complete somersault, and landed back on my feet still running.

Jenn says:

I love the volleyball serve of the same caliber: touching the top of the net and falling onto the other side. Only thing better is the one that jussst hits the line after the other team didn't go for it because they all thought it was going out.

Mike says:

As we say in beer-league hockey . . . the garbage, goal-mouth scramble tip-in can be an end-to-end rush with a backhanded flip that knocks the goalie's water bottle five feet in the air by the time the story is told at the coffee truck the next morning.

Claire says:

Air Hockey Self Score = my primary strategy for playing the game. If I just keep my game tight defensively, eventually my husband will self-score himself into oblivion. A beautiful thing to watch.

Hayley says:

Reminds me of my only proud moment in basketball when I managed to shoot an all-net shot past a defender from thirty or forty feet away. I got a standing ovation from the bleachers and failed to mention I'd actually been aiming for my teammate standing beside the hoop and just wildly missed him.

JP says:

I played competitive soccer for 15 years and I'm a firm believer the flukes are really just the result of intense wanting and willing for success and therefore not flukes at all. They are deliberate interventions of the sports gods showing their true goodness!

Shampoo memories

Shampoo memories are distant scents from days gone by that suddenly waft back into your brain.

Wet moldy cardboard—and you're back in your childhood bedroom closet in the attic of that creaky house with broken board games and Nancy Drews on the floor in that tiny muggy room with the slanted ceiling and cracked floors.

Deodorant beside you on the train—and you're back on the futon in your first boyfriend's basement at two in the morning with staccato breaths while nervously listening for footsteps upstairs.

Putting on an old hand cream—and you're back in your grandma's kitchen, sneaking caramels from the crystal dish, soap operas on in the background, lawn mower buzzing in the backyard.

Shampoo memories offer a new beginning or call back a distant end. Smile as you look back on these memories that built you and made you, **formed you and raised you**, as they reflect back a little scene that shaped your life.

AWESOME!

Chomping up and down a cob of hot, farm-fresh corn like a wild animal

··

I was reading about wolverines.

These raccoon-sized forest dwellers can take down a moose and fight off a **grizzly bear**. They are small but known as one of the most vicious and ferocious animals in the world where they command huge ranges in the northern forests of Canada, Russia, and Scandinavia. Wolverines have large paws, long nails, and sharp teeth, and they bite mercilessly into their prey again and again and again.

They look a lot like you chomping down a cob of hot corn.

Everything in the forest fears you!

Dangerous predator, **ruthless killer**, deadly corn-biter.

You spin the cob and chomp and chomp and chomp some more. Kernels fly in all directions, bits of husk stick to your chin, and when you're finally done everyone watches you stare into the forest with your sharp teeth and dark gums visible and just scream as loud as you can.

Make sure you finish by darting your eyes left, darting your eyes right, and running into the woods, leaving everyone at the picnic table confused and laughing.

AWESOME!

Seeing the delivery truck pull up in the middle of your street and wondering if the Cardboard Box Roulette will land on your porch

....

Whenever I've ordered something online and know it's coming, I'm excited when I see the truck pulling up to the middle of the street and the delivery person start fishing through the jumble of boxes to find the one she's about to bring to me or one of my neighbors.

If it's not for me . . . the anticipation keeps building.

If it is for me . . . it's

AWESOME!

When halfway into a videoconference a cat nobody saw before suddenly wakes up on someone's lap

....

When a cat nobody saw before suddenly wakes up on someone's lap it freezes the meeting in a thought-bubble tableau of everybody suddenly thinking how good a nap would feel right about now. Feels like a tease, but if the cat yawns, **arches its back**, or stretches into a nice long Downward Cat onscreen it gives everyone on the call permission to stop and do a nice long back stretch, too.

Thanks, pussycat.

AWESOME!

When that person you haven't seen in a while doesn't guilt trip you for not seeing them in a while

....

Did you used to get your cheeks pinched?

When I was a kid, Poona Auntie always pinched my cheeks at family gatherings. And as if the death grip on my ruby-browns wasn't enough, she always accompanied it with some classic Indian head wobbles and lines like "Why don't you ever call me, *beta gee*? Why has it been so long? Why don't you ever phone your Poona Auntie?"

Guilt, pain, shame, and a quick feeling of being a bad nephew.

I guess it never struck me to actually take a break from **fighting Hammer Brothers** in my basement to phone up a distant aunt and start gabbing like we were sitting under permers at the beauty salon.

And what would have happened if I did call the aunt whose only conversation topic was how I didn't call her? Would we have suddenly started swapping recipes for **goat vindaloo** or started debating the latest Bollywood star turn? Or would we have simply inched forward a step to discussing how I never came to visit?

In my early twenties I ran a sandwich shop and sometimes had customers walk in who I hadn't seen in a while. What did

I say to them? "Hey, where have you been? Why don't you visit your favorite sandwich shop anymore?"

I noticed when I said that they'd quickly flash an apologetic smile, order a turkey-bacon-guacamole, and then disappear forever. I would hear the door ding shut and almost see the swirling **cloud of shame** hovering over them as they climbed inside their dented Honda Civic and drove straight out of my life.

It took time to realize the shame was because of me.

And that it was undeserved.

I had become the Poona Auntie of Sandwiches.

Why did those customers never come back? Same reason I never called my aunt. Who can handle that kind of guilt? Much easier to disappear completely.

Shame clouds came those days because I wasn't confident. "I'm a non-caller, I'm a bad nephew, I'm not holding up my end of the relationship."

I hadn't realized yet that the **snow globe lives** we live just shake us all sideways. And that's okay. That's normal. No one is to blame. Neither one of us is a bad person.

Guilt tripping is just emotional lashing out. People who feel more hurt when receiving criticism from partners are more likely to respond dramatically to make their partner feel guilty. **Hurt people hurt people.** When you say, "We haven't seen each other in a while," you're usually also saying, "And it's all your fault."

But we all live in the snow globe.

We shake up, shake down, fly sideways, fly around. Sometimes the shakes send us flying endlessly. Doesn't mean we did anything wrong. We are all just growing to slowly appreciate what we had and **what we have**. We can learn to let go a little more of what could or should be.

We have moments, days, this year . . . right here.

Tomorrows are never guaranteed so no need to soak them with Poona Auntie sayings or spray shame clouds over people when all you really mean to say is:

"I am so glad to see you."

"I feel lucky to have this."

"Thank you for being in my life."

"And thank you for being
AWESOME!

Actually making the right amount of spaghetti

....

AWESOME!

Midnight summer walks

Step into the breeze.

After the sun dips down the houselights flick on and streets fill with windows of checkery yellow teeth. Playgrounds start to empty and distant barking dogs fill the air before moonbeams start shining on tree branches, warm winds whisper through **black hedges**, and a warm and soothing softness settles over everything like a blanket.

Joggers race inside and dog walkers head home as you walk past garden silhouettes and locked shops on quieter and quieter streets.

Midnight summer walks sit in the sacred space between today and tomorrow. Systems shut down, **stresses ease up**, and work fades as you stroll through empty streets and quiet paths after dark.

Drift from today . . . let the world fade away.

Nothing else matters right now.

AWESOME!

Becoming friends with the only other kid who doesn't know anyone here

Dragged to mom's book club because the babysitter canceled you were expecting a warm cup of grape juice and four boring hours in someone's rocking-chair-and-doily-filled living room. But then another misplaced kid arrives! Since they also have no intention of **sipping chardonnay** while discussing underlying themes of disenfranchisement in the latest Pulitzer Prize winner, you decide to bond for an afternoon full of laughs while watching TV.

Circumstances threw your friendship together, but that doesn't mean it's not real. Life is short, delicate, and fleeting and convenience-bonding is good for the soul.

Use your old jokes, **be a New You**, and enjoy some fragile but loving moments with someone you've never met.

AWESOME!

Somehow finishing your shampoo and conditioner bottles at the same time

The strings go up an octave and the choir hits the upper register as all the planets suddenly align in a moment of true Shower Destiny.

AWESOME!

When the categories in *Jeopardy!* are right in your wheelhouse

"Rhymes with Brown"
"Sports Ending with Ball"
"Name That Ocean"
"Served with Fries"
"How Many Wheels?"
    AWESOME!

Flipping over your grilled cheese to discover you perfectly cooked the bottom side

....

Can you cook with your eyes closed?

True stovetop mastery is cooking without looking.

My mom does that when she makes Indian food. Glugs oil in a pot, finely chops a white onion, and then you may as well blindfold her because the aloo gobi just appears half an hour later. Turmeric and **garam masala** shaken in, tomato and garlic added, cauliflower and potatoes chopped, and she carries on a conversation without breaking eye contact the whole time.

This cooking-without-looking trait must have skipped a generation because when I cook I'm squinting at recipes, cracking eggs all over my hands, and getting stressed as **oven timers beep** and pots boil over.

Grilled cheese should be a breeze, but I often find myself **chiseling cold butter**, spreading holes on the bread, and then tossing it butter-side-down in a frying pan before coming back to flip the whole thing over a few minutes later when it's either still light brown and buttery-wet or instead horribly black-burnt to a crisp.

That's what makes it so sweet when I flip the grilled cheese at the perfect time with those brown crispy marks that seem to smile at me and say:

"You're one step closer to doing this with your eyes closed."

AWESOME!

The Sniff Test

Works on underwear, milk, and babies.

If it smells bad, it's bad. If it smells good, it's AWESOME!

Finally cleaning your disgustingly filthy windshield

After momentarily blinding yourself under a thick layer of **muddy wiper smears**, you suddenly gaze out with fast-blinking eyes and a dropped jaw through a crystal clear half circle of heavenly road ahead.

It's like getting a new pair of eyes.

AWESOME!

When your completely plugged-up nostrils suddenly open up with no warning

....

Nose, what's your deal?

I've been frustrated all morning with your **snotty head-clogging ways**. Breathing wasn't happening and I was left mouth-gasping for air every few seconds to bypass your invisible, impenetrable wall.

You remember when I tried blowing my skull into some tissues to clear your salty barricade, right? All I got for my troubles was wet tissue up my nose and sore eyeballs from the pressure.

So I gave up! **I gave in.** I gave it a good shot.

What choice did I have but slump my shoulders, curl my lips down, and move on?

But after spending the day **wrestling down my defenses**, you decided to just completely out of nowhere . . . open! Without warning! You burst the dam without a memo to the foreman. A gale-force wind sucked into my nose and flooded my lungs and the weight of the world was lifted.

I sucked in deep breaths, I sucked in cool air, but more than that?

I sucked in . . . a new life.

AWESOME!

"I did a great 'lesson' with a grade eight class at my school. I showed them awesome things and then the kids made a list of their own and presented their ideas to the class. Here are our favorites:

> Running through the ribbon after a race
> Giving an expensive gift that you got for free
> Jumping off your roof into a pool
> Blowing out someone else's birthday candles
> When live performers fall off the stage
> Finding a chocolate bar in your pocket that you think
>   is melted then finding out it's not
> The smell of blankets and mints at Grandma's house
> Watching a scary movie during a thunderstorm in
>   the dark
> The feeling you have after receiving a compliment
> Teachers losing test papers
> The day you graduate
> Finding something in your size on an end of season
>   sale rack
> Hiding something in your friend's afro
> The first chip in the bag
> Counting the stars in the sky

Jumping in a pool with your clothes on
The first swing of summer
Screaming as loud as you can on a roller coaster

Hope you enjoy these awesome things!!!"

—Ms. Peters and Taylor, Marysuzan, Natalie, Jenn,
Matt R., Matt H., Josh, Cody, Mitan, TJ, Joey,
Kareem, Brooke, Najah, Lavan, Odane,
Zakk, Brad, Naser, Hannah, Tausha, Rachell,
Laura, and Amy at Templemead School

Putting things in your shoe so you don't forget them later

I am forgetful.

Keys in my pants, food in my microwave, words at the end of my.

If you've ever tapped **empty pockets** in front of your locked front door in the middle of the night you know exactly how painful forgetfulness can be.

Fortunately we live in a bright and modern **Future World** where decades of cutting-edge research has resulted in breakthrough technological advances to help give us a way to remember everything we would otherwise leave behind.

I'm talking about throwing it in your shoe, people.

Yes, it's an ingenious and foolproof research-backed system for helping your **Future Self** whenever you think your **Current Self** might leave something behind.

Putting things in your shoe so you don't forget them later.

Works for everything except raw eggs, origami, and tacks.

AWESOME!

The sound of a golf ball falling into the cup

....

I was the Mini Golf King.

Yes, back in those **blurry '80s** there wasn't a course that could trip me up. Slippery slopes, puddle patches, shady piles of windswept maple keys were no match for my well-practiced whacking of those **neon-pink balls**. Smack it off the chewed-up black mat, bounce it off the windmill arm, and let it slide down the hill and right into the hole.

That was my game.

The sound of a golf ball falling into the cup is the sound of satisfaction. Whether you just finished **chipping through the rough** or twelve-putting your way to the finish line, it really doesn't matter.

That final shot always sounds the same.

It's the sound of satisfaction going down the drain.

AWESOME!

Blaming your fart on the dog

Thanks for taking the heat, Rusty.
   AWESOME!

Actually finding time to eat whatever I want

....

I have been a sole parent for all of my child's twenty-one years. I have been mother, father, policeman, counselor, chief, cook, and bottle washer. My son still lives at home so in between his studies and work there is little time for him to spend cooking. So as I am the "best cook in the world" according to him, it's left to me! But now that he's starting to spend some time traveling with his sports team, I get to eat two-minute noodles for a week if I want to with all sorts of weird things like soda crackers and peanuts and barbecue sauce poured in. And for me this is great because I HATE COOKING!

AWESOME!

—*Subhada Das, Fremantle, Australia*

Going to the movies by yourself

My first time was an accident.

I was fourteen years old and got to the theater too late to meet my friends. I walked down the aisles awkwardly **whisper-yelling** in the dark and when I didn't find them I just settled into a seat by myself at the back.

It felt strange sitting alone at the movies for the first time, but you know what? I also loved it. And I learned a few things about the value of going out on the town solo, such as:

1. **Dressing down for Chinatown.** When you're chilling at home under the blanket you can relax in sweats, but when you're hitting the town it's time for tight denim and scrunchy shoes. When you're going solo, you can ignore the Fashion Police and enjoy the rom-com in your maroon sweatpants and tank top.

2. **Kicking open the escape hatch.** When you're lugging your little brother to a Saturday afternoon cartoon or trying to be romantic by letting your date pick the Friday night show, well, the escape hatch is bolted on tight. But if you're watching a movie alone and aren't digging the flick, you can just bail and see something else guilt free. Freedom is always nearby.

3. **Squeezing into center seats.** You know when you're looking for two seats in a packed theater but there's

only ever like one random seat in the middle of a long row somewhere? Well, now that single seat is yours! Forget the horrible front row and just wedge yourself in.

4. **Invest in yourself.** Sure, we're social primates who love dinner parties, basement hangouts, and incessant group texting . . . but it's also good to learn to enjoy your own company while deepening your sense of self-awareness, self-worth, and self-confidence.

Going to the movies by yourself is about growing up, growing older, and growing more comfortable in your own skin.
Punch your ticket to a wonderful night.
AWESOME!

Getting tiny chores done before the microwave beeps

....

Beat the beep.

Toss that bowl of instant oatmeal, **can of ravioli**, or salty plate of last night's stir-fry in the microwave and get ready for sixty seconds of tornado-twisting action in the kitchen. When the door slams and the glass starts turning, it's time to start scrubbing the last few dirty dishes, tie up the garbage, or speed-fold all the towels.

Now when the oatmeal bings, burning ravioli dings, or soy-smeared broccoli rings, you'll enjoy your meal a little more knowing you maximized your time. The microwave timer gave you a countdown of energy so now as you settle into your couch dent in front of the TV just wipe the **sweaty bangs** off your face and chow down feeling sixty seconds more productive and a whole lot more

AWESOME!

When that mandatory after-work hangout planned by HR is canceled by HR

....

We've been working hard all day.
   Thanks for letting us go home.
   AWESOME!

Tennis grunts

Tennis is classy.

Fans don't paint their faces silver, **put on a pair of horns**, or stand shirtless waving cardboard signs while chugging from Beer Hats. No, tennis fans sit in hushed crowds, whisper politely, and eat berries and cream in front of the Royal Box.

Players are classy, too, with supermodel good looks, **designer clothes**, and sports skirts. With hushed announcers, **soldier-straight ball boys**, and serious coaches in fancy sunglasses, tennis sometimes seems less like a sport and more like a dinner party.

That is until the grunting kicks in.

Tennis grunts fill the stuffy air with hilarious animal noises. Gorilla grunts are suddenly all you hear above squeaky shoes, **clinking jewelry**, and whispery gasps. Tennis grunts remind us we're human, they remind us we're watching a sport, and they give us a smile when we all need more smiles and we think that's enough to be

AWESOME!

Successfully firing your shopping cart thirty feet across the parking lot before it perfectly crashes into all the other carts

AWESOME!

Facial hair experiments

I used to be The Wolf Man.

At least, that's what a big guy named Fletch called me in tenth grade homeroom. He said it with a **hearty, bug-eyed giggle** while tugging the soft patches of thin black hair extending down my neck from my jaw to my collarbone.

Now, I wasn't just born The Wolf Man. No, I had to create the identity by first working up the courage to trim my thin, soft mustache and sideburns for the first time. That first shave was a nerve-racking ordeal with a fresh razor, steamy mirror, too much lather, and too much blood.

And I guess being around fifteen years old and new to this whole **slicing the hair off your face with a knife** thing, I didn't realize that you were supposed to shave the whole neck area, too. So I didn't get the neck area. I completely missed the neck area. And for a good couple of weeks, I walked around the high school with a smooth, freshly shorn face, and an untamed, hairy neck area.

Ar-ar-aroooooooo!

But you know, looking back, I really do miss it. I probably couldn't pull off the **Gratuitously Hairy Neck** look these days, unless I wanted to become a mountain guide, deep-sea fisherman, or scarf warmer-upper for the ultra rich.

And it's not just the Hairy Neck look that deserves mention, either. There are so many other classic facial hair experiments that deserve a shout-out:

1. **Muttonchops.** Famous muttonchoppers include Elvis Presley, Neil Young, and Wolverine. Although it seems obvious, muttonchops are so named because they look just like big lamb chops. How do you grow a pair? Easy, just ignore trimming your sideburns for a decade.

2. **The Chin Strap.** This chin strap is a deep study in the art of making perfect lines with a sharp razor. It shows form, style, and patience, because nobody can really nail it without messing it up a few times first and shaving the whole thing off in frustration. The chin strap goes in and (mostly) out of fashion but can provide a nice base to a goatee. Pairs well with souped-upped, low-riding Acuras.

3. **Weird Beards.** Ever see someone who can't grow a beard just go ahead and grow one anyway? That splotchy monster deserves respect.

4. **Soul Patches.** A soul patch is a small patch of facial hair just above the chin and just below the lips. Did you know the soul patch became popular with jazz musicians in the '50s because it provided a nice, comfy place to rest the trumpet?

5. **Horseshoe Mustache.** There's some overlap here with the bushier Handlebar and the generally longer Fu Manchu, but either way we're talking about

a full-grown mustache that slides down to the chin to make a complete horseshoe. Very difficult to pull off unless you're a bartender at a dive bar, cowboy, or Hulk Hogan.

6. **Too Much Time on Your Hands.** This is an intricate and detailed facial hair involving lightning bolts or abstract images that look like they're from a Spirograph. Most of them don't last longer than an afternoon, but they're great conversation pieces.

I miss the youthful freedom of **bizarre, anything-goes facial hair** because there's something so liberating, creatively satisfying, and fiercely expressive about experimenting with your face and a hot blade in front of a steamy bathroom mirror.

No matter how crooked your chin strap, puny your mutton-chops, or splotchy your weird beard, whatever you've got going on is something we declare to be

AWESOME!

"A dozen years ago I signed up for Big Sisters and was matched with Tiffany, an 11-year-old creative spirit. We bonded instantly and spent many hours together doing awesome things. We lost touch for years but Tiff called out of the blue one day and we reconnected like there hadn't been a gap. Friendships that make the leap over years of space are truly awesome. Well, Tiff has now grown into a beautiful young woman and I just watched her graduate from college with tears of pride in my eyes. I gave her *The Book of Awesome* as a present and tucked comments into all the pages that rang true for us. I even tucked money into 'Finding money in your old coat pocket' and then added a line about how it's awesome to randomly find money in a book as well."

—Sandy

Being suddenly really into bird watching

Level 1: Beginner. A tiny bird in a backyard tree catches your eye. Black and white feathers, hopping up a shriveled trunk, maybe a smear of red on its head? What is it? Do you still have those old binoculars in the basement? You rush down to grab them, but when you get back it's gone. You notice you care, though. You're interested. The binoculars stay at the ready.

Level 2: Amateur. Few days later you see another bird in the tree. You grab the binoculars. Brown back, white breast, looks like . . . a sparrow. Yes. Are there different kinds of sparrows? What kind is it? How do you tell the difference? Wait, another bird jumps into view. Small. Jumpy. White body. Black hat. Gone. Will it return? You feel the excitement building.

Level 3: Novice. You tell a friend into birds that you think you saw a Black-Capped Chickadee but you're not sure. She lends you her bird book. You start flipping. Oh! That first bird you saw was a woodpecker! Downy? Hairy? What's a Pileated Woodpecker? Or a Northern Flicker? There are so many! You start a list: Downy Woodpecker? House Sparrow? Black-Capped Chickadee. Getting serious.

Level 4: Pro. You toss the binoculars in your bag and decide to spend lunch at the downtown park instead of at your desk at the office. You eat on a bench between tall pine trees. Northern Cardinal! Something small and yellow? Something . . . plain gray? With a long tail? You flip through your book. Maybe an American Goldfinch? And a Northern Mockingbird? Maybe not? You're getting the hang of this. You feel a connection, a sense of calm. You slowly start feeling part of something much bigger than yourself. You wonder how many birds you've seen before you started to notice them.

Level 5: Expert. You start mentioning bits of bird trivia to friends. "Did you know a mockingbird can mimic hundreds of sounds? Gulls, crows, even a beeping garbage truck?" You start calling your list of birds a "life list" and see your number hit ten then fifty then a hundred. You fall down online rabbit holes reading about the ninety-million-year history of the Common Loon or the pole-to-pole migration of the Arctic Tern. You feel a little less tethered to our species and more connected to living things in general. You wonder if you're going to end up like the pigeon lady in *Mary Poppins*. You fall asleep singing about tuppence, tuppence, tuppence a baaaaaaaaaag . . .

Level 6: Master. You start hanging out on online birder channels and go on a weekend trip with a friend to catch the migration. Cooper's Hawk, Blackburnian Warbler, Wood Duck! You start recognizing birdcalls and identifying birds before you see them. A friend shows you a grainy photo of a bird in their backyard saying they *think* it's a chickadee but they're not sure. You lend them your book and decide to get them binoculars for their birthday.

AWESOME!

That person at the table who suddenly convinces everyone to get dessert

....

At the end of a belly-bursting meal the server pops by to ask if anyone wants coffee or dessert, and that's when it's time for the classic three-second **Dessert Pause** where everybody suddenly stares around the table squinting and sizing each other up. Nobody wants to make the fateful first move and be the lone **Cheesecake Ranger** who delays everybody getting home and, at the same time, nobody wants to be the wet blanket who poo-poos the party.

That's why we salute the person who cracks first.

"You know what, yeah—I'll take the massive seven-layer Chocolate Death Blow, please. Hmm, sorry? No, no, just one fork is fine."

The scales have tipped!

There is now only one thing that can correct this massive dessert imbalance.

Death Blows for everyone!

AWESOME!

When you owe someone $20 and someone else owes you $20 but then they just give $20 to the person you owe instead

....

Way to cut out the middleman.
    AWESOME!

The sound of a bouncing basketball echoing around the playground as the sun sets

With birds singing from hydro wires, mosquitoes swirling over darkening grass fields, and children silhouetting on the slides.
AWESOME!

Feeling it in your bones

....

Born and blasted into the world you're a baby brain with wide eyes, chubby legs, and cloudy thoughts. Mom lifts you and picks you, eyes open and close, fogs rise and settle. Tears stream and **faces scream** as your swirling brain twists and turns into thoughts.

Nothing makes sense till it does.

Nothing feels right till it does.

Chalk raps on blackboards beside times tables, language stirs sounds into sentences, stories send you flying into faraway worlds. Book reports and homework inspections, **chemistry labs** and biology dissections, all fill your spinning brain with numbers and theories and thoughts . . .

Nothing makes sense till it does.

Nothing feels right till it does.

Teenage sleepovers and late-night walks, summertime camps and suppertime talks, keep expanding your mind and your understanding of the world. First kisses and first blushes, first fights and first touches, all fill your heart with dreams, expand your brain's bookshelf, and get you thinking about a life outside the story of yourself.

Nothing makes sense till it does.

Nothing feels right till it does.

But sometimes challenging lectures and scattering friends, confusing debates without exams at the end can frighten your mind or scare dreams away, can fracture some feelings or muddy things today. Family pressures and **social graces**, broken promises from trusted faces might suddenly swish you upside down, scatter your thoughts, or dim your heart.

When nothing makes sense . . .

When nothing feels right . . .

When it gets scary to realize . . .

There are no instructions in life . . .

Now you hit the end of this moment and it's time to open your eyes and look behind you, and as you stare ahead to the next it's time to open your heart and look inside you.

Because today you're right here . . .

And there's so far to go . . .

And today there's still fear . . .

But there's only one way to know . . .

Feel it in your bones.

Feel it in your bones.

Feel it in your bones.

Feel your bones to move forward, feel your bones to move on, feel your bones to forget, feel your bones to carry on. Feel your bones to say you're sorry, feel your bones to show you care, feel your bones to choose tomorrow, feel those bones to get you there.

So whatever you're thinking about today . . . stop trying to choose and choose.

Whatever you're wondering about today . . . just look inside for clues.

Yes, whatever you're worrying about . . . just stop and feel instead.

Because when you feel it in your bones you can smile and forget your head.

AWESOME!

The blanket

No offense fire, wheel, or printing press.

But blankets are the greatest technology ever invented.

There we were—naked in the plains, shivering in the rains—when one of our **Cave Great-Great Grandparents** had the brilliant idea of just tearing off another animal's fur and draping it over ourselves.

Was it polite? No. Did it do the job? Still does!

We have used **Blanket Technology** for hundreds of thousands of years and they truly offer us so much:

1. **Instant protection.** When you're a kid, blankets fend off monsters and prevent robbers from seeing you. Also, blankets give newborn babies a sense of security, warmth, and closeness that feels like the womb. That's probably why most of us still sleep with a blanket every night . . . even when it's hot. Are you a frantic, flailing baby without your blanket, too? I absolutely am.

2. **Release the flame within.** When I was a kid I didn't realize our bodies were giving off so much heat until a teacher had us breathe into our hands and feel the warmth. We are all little fires—heating up rooms, coffee shops, and planets. Blankets help capture that heat and, yes, blanket ourselves in it. In a way every

piece of clothing is a little blanket. Sure, they may be shaped into underwear, sweatshirts, and skullcaps now, but everything started out as a bear pelt.

3. **Saving money, saving ourselves.** Cranking thermostats fills the atmosphere with billowing fumes that warm our planet. A vote for the blanket is a vote for the future. Blankets never expire, fade away, or go out of style. They don't need outlets, batteries, or version upgrades. I'm guessing you have a blanket that you've had since you can remember. Was it your mom's? Her mom's? There's no reason anybody should throw out a blanket. Remember: They last a long time, so we last a long time, too.

Sorry fire, wheel, and printing press.
Sorry telescopes, bricks, and glass.
Sorry cars, computers, and cell phones.
One invention has you all outclassed.
AWESOME!

COMMENTS:

....

Kathy says:

Blankets are fantastic for so many things! Definitely used mine to hide from monsters and robbers, making living room tents, and dressing up in a swirling princess dress. No curtains for that first apartment or dorm room? Just throw a blanket over the rod!

Jen replies:

Blanket forts are the best! I made one when I was 30 big enough for the three people and two cats in my house.

Sheila says:

Last Christmas my sister gave me the most hilarious zebra-print fake fur blanket. So cheesy, I sort of inwardly rolled my eyes until I touched it. It was so soft and comforting. Now I snatch it every night. My five-year-old loves it, too. Also, I quilt. Making oneself a blanket one can then use is pretty awesome, too.

Jason says:

A 1-sentence personal story: When you're homeless, sleeping in the park under a tree, in the rain, blankets take on a whole new meaning, and you can't help but appreciate them on a level that is almost magical. God, I love blankets.

JT says:

I am now officially crawling back into my bed.

When your footsteps line up perfectly with the floor tiles you're walking across right now

Brain, you're funny.

Who knows what cavemen electronics fire you up on a daily basis? Something must have been hardwired a while back to make us love popping bubble wrap, **cracking thin frozen puddles** on cold mornings, and pushing in those little circle buttons on top of the McDonald's cup.

Clicks clack, **neurons snap**, brain cells buzz, and smiles attack whenever those feel-good jabs start feel-good jabbing.

When footsteps line up perfectly with the black and white floor tiles, it's like the **stars are aligning** for a surprise twenty seconds of fun. Perfectly avoiding all sidewalk cracks, squeezing through a door as it's shutting without touching it, and walking onto an escalator without slowing down your stride all come close to the feeling of **Checkerboard Stepping** through that snobby lobby.

Smile as the buttoned-up front-desk staff stares in awe, **drops their jaws**, and bursts into applause.

Because you just nailed it, friend.

Right when it mattered most.

AWESOME!

The Honor System

....

I grew up riding shotgun a lot.

My dad was a teacher so summers were spent fiddling with the **radio dial** as we dropped my mom off at work, took my sister to swimming lessons, and waited in bank lineups.

Since bank machines weren't invented yet, those lineups were long and slow ordeals: filling out wispy-thin slips of paper, winding through velvet ropes, inch by inch, minute by minute.

That might be why I could probably still give a **police sketch artist** a vivid description of what the inside of a bank looked like, right down to thin black carpets, giant unhinged vault door with dead bolts the size of tennis ball containers, and, of course, the paper box of foil-wrapped mint chocolates on the counter with a little change box collecting money for veterans.

I don't remember wondering how the veterans got into the mint chocolate business, but I was curious why their little chocolates sat **out in the open** where anybody could grab them.

Little did I realize then that **The Honor System** really is great for at least three big reasons:

1. **Pennies from heaven.** Imagine a world where we don't need systems to check for trust—no jail bars on pharmacy windows, security cameras outside corner stores, or metal detectors on the steps of the high

school. The Honor System skips the locks in favor of trust. We all win.

2. **Hit the fast lane.** Since The Honor System relies on trust it also moves us a lot faster through our clogged-up cattle pen security checks, body scans, and baggage inspections. There's no scanning items through systems, printing out endless receipt tapes, and filing everything with the government a year later. It's just done. It's just easy.

3. **Embraces our humanity.** Sure, there are a few bad eggs, but most people won't snag a foil-wrapped mint chocolate without paying. It doesn't feel honorable! The Honor System fires up our moral compass to guide us from the inside without all the red lights and blaring signs telling us what to do outside.

Let's take a moment to say thanks to The Honor System. Let's hear it for "Pay what you can" night at the **Comedy Club**, $5 Friday Jeans Day buckets at the office, wooden shelves of peaches on the side of the country road with a tin can for payment . . . and little boxes of mint chocolates everywhere.

No offense Buddy, Metric, or Solar.

But Honor's got you beat.

AWESOME!

COMMENTS:

Wendy says:

A flower booth on a farm in the Okanagan Valley in British Columbia, where beautiful fresh cut bouquets are available, spring through fall. We've been told by the owners they were able to put their kids through college on the honor system manned flower booth . . .

Key replies:

I saw one of those last year in a public park in Zurich and it blew my mind! You could cut your own flowers with the pruning shears left in the booth. There was a price list with prices for each flower, and you put money in a box after making your bouquet.

Kim says:

You had me right until you said that the honor system is better than the buddy system! I'm a camp counselor, so "Take a buddy" is one of my most oft-spoken sentences! I love the buddy system! All of a sudden just because you have another kid you can venture so much further. But I will agree the honor system is equivalent to the buddy system!!!

Deborah says:

I live in Iowa. Along our roads it is often corn, tomatoes, and zucchini. Sometimes the zucchini is actually free, there is so much of it. What a simpler society with the honor system.

That person who hands you a tissue when you're out somewhere with an endlessly dripping nose

....

It can happen anywhere.

Waiting in line for a coffee, writing a two-hour exam, or just walking down the hallway at work, it suddenly hits you that you need to blow your nose and you need to blow it now.

You tap your pockets, check your purse, but no luck. You have no tissues. You have no napkins. You are alone.

Your nose twitches and tickles and drips and dribbles and you're suddenly shoved onstage as a squeaky curtain rises and stage lights blind your eyes. Welcome to the Off-Off-Broadway performance of *That Drippy Emergency*!

Today you're the star of the show:

Act 1: Sleeve Sliding. Welcome back to sixth grade. You slide your slippery snout across your dirty, fraying sweatshirt sleeve. You just bought yourself a 25-second reprieve before you figure out what to do next.

Act 2: The Big Snort. It's time to get your head in the game. Here's where you look left and right to confirm nobody is listening and then yank your head up fast while snorting as loud as possible. A big dose of dust and some crisp winter breeze zooms in there to chill your brain. The Big Snort isn't pretty, but hey, you're just reading your lines.

Act 3: Wet Lips. Sleeves and snorts fail to stop the rush, so eventually we get a scene of you staring around frantically while the rushing comes! The dam breaks, the river gushes, and now you're a three-year-old running around at recess.

Act 4: The Replacement Player. Your brain kicks in to help. You need to blow and you need to blow right now. So what do you do? Rapidly investigate all premises for anything resembling a tissue. Scratchy brown paper towel? Piece of white paper from the laser printer? Squeezed-and-folded toilet paper roll? Whatever you find, that's what you use.

Yes, if you've ever starred in the one-person show of *That Drippy Emergency* you know it's not a great role. The pay is zero, the hours are terrible, and you finish every performance a slobbery mess.

That's why it's great when someone sees you struggling onstage and quietly slips you a tissue.

Today we give thanks to the offstage director who steps in to save the show.

AWESOME!

Slowly shifting back to Nature Time

It was a dumb idea.

I was two months into the first real relationship after my divorce. Leslie and I were falling in love, but then I suddenly had a two-week trip on the horizon just as we were starting into seeing-each-other-every-day status.

By the time I reached the final few days of my trip, I was missing her so much. I was in **Hong Kong** and we were video-calling in the middle of my nights. And during one of these calls, I said something like "I don't want to be jet-lagged when I get home because then I'll be sleeping all day when you're awake and I'll miss you so much, so I have decided to go completely nocturnal for the few days I have left."

"Nocturnal? That's not going to work," she said.

"No, no, it will, it will," I said. "I'll even figure which hours to sleep on the flight so when I land it'll be your morning *and* my morning and then we can spend the day together and the next day and the next day and the next day and the next day and the n—"

"This is a bad idea," she said, shaking her head.

However, in some kind of **deranged romantic gesture** I in-sisted on it. Hong Kong is such a bustling city and Joey, the old roommate I was staying with, was always busy until late at work, so he could never hang out till 11:00 p.m. anyway.

For the next few days, Joey and I went for dinner until the

wee hours of the morning. When we got back to his apartment, I'd call Leslie. She taught eighth graders at an inner-city school and would get home and flip on her computer screen while she cooked. I was entranced watching her **chop onions** or whip up a batch of brownies to take to her students the next day.

After our call, I bridged myself till morning however I could before spectacularly crashing on an air mattress while the sun rose over smog-covered high-rises and slipped through closed blinds.

I thought I had a foolproof plan.

But it failed spectacularly.

Mother Nature slapped my circadian rhythms silly and when I landed back at home I felt nauseous and foggy for weeks. My waking and sleeping schedules felt even more out of whack than if I hadn't tried messing with them beforehand.

I guess nature and our bodies sync for a reason. We feed off the same energy sources and we've been doing it for millions of years. What's new? Lightbulbs! Extending day into night might help us get more done, but endlessly glowing screens jolt our senses long into the night. Bright screens late at night delay the onset of a natural late-night **energy burst**, which for millions of years helped us scurry back to the cave and start the fire in the dark.

Late-night screens mock our evolutionary history by reducing melatonin production for a restful sleep. Sometimes after we toss and turn we strap even more technology to ourselves in a frantic attempt to right some wrong that's really only solved by acceptance.

The planet has been spinning for billions of years and will

hopefully keep spinning for billions more. In our brief flickers of consciousness sometimes we face the sun . . . and sometimes we don't. Winds settle, darkness falls, and it feels good to settle and fall alongside it.

"I might have told you that," Leslie has reminded me many times since.

It's a lesson I'm still learning.

Letting ourselves slow down into **Nature Time** helps our bodies get closer to being part of the earth . . . rather than just standing on top of it.

AWESOME!

Anything really, really heavy

I was around ten years old when I successfully begged my parents for some tiny gadget from Radio Shack that let me play **LCD checkers** in the backseat of the wood-paneled station wagon. The thing was like Game Boy's Great Grandpa or something, but after I fought with scissors to break it out of its carbonite-like shell I remember thinking, "Uh oh, this thing is really light."

Sure enough a few King Mes later and the LCD checkers machine went kaput. Turns out it didn't just feel like plastic-wrapped air with a rusty circuit board wedged inside—that's what it was. It got me thinking there's just something better about anything really, really heavy.

Yes, in these days of bendable, breakable, and throwaway there's something decidedly beautiful about anything really, really heavy.

Like for instance:

- **Old toys from Grandpa's basement.** When you come across wooden trucks or heavy paddles it's time to slow down and sink into a Sunday afternoon. Keep fishing through boxes and you might find a solid metal xylophone, an old train set, or a doll with one eyelid permanently closed and a rock-hard head that doubles as a club for that pre-dinner battle with your brother.

- **Small appliances.** What was the greatest toaster oven you ever owned? Heavy, small, metal, crusty black inside, and maybe the door didn't close all the way, but it toasted toast perfectly every time? And when that old lumbering beast finally croaked it caused deep grief because you never found one as good, right? Me too.

- **Pens.** Bottom of the barrel are flimsy four-inch plastic yellow ones that clip onto your mini-golf card. Top of the heap is that heavy metal one with the feather lying beside the guest book at the wedding reception.

- **Pile of blankets.** Have you ever stepped down a friend's rickety staircase into the cold, unfinished basement where you'll be sleeping tonight? If so, you know the deep joy when your friend walks down a few minutes later with a tall pile of heavy blankets. Time to lie back and let them layer you like a lasagna.

- **Old, dangerous playground equipment.** Burning hot slides, squeaky metal see-saws, and rusty 200-pound merry-go-rounds beat flimsy plastic slides, tiny rocking horses, and anything made of foam.

- **Unwrapped Christmas presents.** Heavy boxes crank up the mystery on Christmas morning and add a lot of value by loudly declaring, "This is not a gift card."

- **Oganesson.** Poor Mendeleev didn't leave a spot for this synthetic element—also known as the last square on the periodic table and the heaviest element on earth. Packing 118 protons into an atom isn't easy, but the result is worth its weight in gold. Actually 39 protons more than gold.

- **Babies.** What's one of the first things people tell you when they have a new baby? How much it weighs. We've been taking weight as an early proxy for health for thousands of years. Clearly, we like our babies with big wobbly heads and lots of fat rolls.
- **Things made of glass.** Plastic Jeep windows, Styrofoam cups, stained yogurt containers, your days are numbered. When we switch plastic for glass, we gain quality.

Heavy means your action figure won't break next week.

Heavy means the omelet is packed with cheese.

Heavy means this was put together by someone . . . who cared.

AWESOME!

COMMENTS:

....

Kathy says:

I'm adding old fridges! I have an old fridge and it is a great heavy thing that holds so many other heavy things I love: milk, wine, cheese, grapes, pepper jelly, cream cheese, bacon, eggs, chocolate pudding, and so much more!

Paula replies:

Got a new washer this year . . . took one young guy to bring the new one down into the basement . . . took two to struggle to get the 35-year-old one up the stairs.

Jdurley says:

My mom was cleaning out a drawer of old stuff and un-earthed some glasses my dad wore in the '70s. It was crazy how heavy they were! Yes, before the super-lightweight, slim, unbreakable, plastic whatevers we have now, glasses were made of . . . wait for it . . . GLASS. And they were thick. And heavy. And slid down your nose. And those heavy glass glasses that slid down your nose gave us the classic nerd move—the one-finger glasses pushup.

Stephanie says:

And when you pulled out one of those heavy marbles in the middle of a marbles match with your mates you were considered superior . . . almost superhuman. You would just hear groans when you pulled it out for your friends knew the time had come for their feeble normal-sized marbles to be smashed into next week.

Val says:

I would add watches. Something about a good, solid, heavy watch sits well with my soul.

Jalus says:

An endearing part of my memories is the heavy rocking chair my grandmother sat in to do her knitting, read me a story, and rock me to sleep. My grandfather used it to smoke his pipe and sit silently watching the fire dance on many a cold winter's night.

The moment at the bar when everyone starts singing together

....

It's a rare moment of unity that goes down one of three ways:

1. **Sports cheer.** We're watching the home team on the big screen. When that final goal is scored and the clock clicks down, it's time to grab each other's shoulders, sway side to side, and let the tears stream down our painted faces.

2. **Birthday fraternity.** It's somebody else's birthday, but the rousing rendition gets everybody in the bar chiming in. It's usually perfect until those last two lines, which come out something like "Happy BIRTH-day *dear* girl-at-the-barrrrrrrrr . . . Happy birthday to youuuuuuuuu."

3. **Late-night sing-a-long.** We're chatting into the early morning when the DJ suddenly drops a fan favorite and cranks it up to unite the crowd for a few minutes before the end of the night. Fists pump to the sky as we spill our plastic cups in this final sloshing screamfest.

Yes, the moment at the bar when everyone starts singing together is a sign that we really are halfway there.

Take my hand. We'll make it . . . I swear.

AWESOME!

Finishing your last exam and starting summer vacation

AWESOME!

The very first bite into a fresh piece of gum

....

It's always the sweetest.

1. **Chiclet Style.** It's time to crush that hard outer white shell into a hundred little pieces. You can do the first bite with your two front teeth (aka The Bugs Bunny) or get your molars in the game from the beginning. Either way, the first bite is your chance to scrape the super-minty shards around inside your mouth before they dissolve and leave you with a thousand remaining chews of flavorless taffy.
2. **Hubba Bubba Style.** Does your dentist put that mouthguard full of goopy fluoride on your teeth like mine does? That's sort of what the first bite of cube-style gum feels like. You can actually pull the gum out after biting down on it and see a perfect imprint of your molars. It feels like a forest ranger picking up animal tracks in the mud.
3. **Juicy Fruit Stick Style.** When you have a long, flat, thin piece of gum, it's important to always curl it onto your tongue like in old TV commercials. The taste-the-taste-the-taste is gonna *mo-ove* ya!

4. **Bazooka Joe Style.** Small rectangular pieces of pink rock-hard gum are the worst. Sure, you get a little comic strip, but that first bite might shatter your teeth. Try tenderizing it first with a spiky wooden mallet.

We've been chewing gum for over a hundred thousand years, so let's take a moment to nod back at our **Cave-Grandparents** for passing along the tradition, because there's a simple joy that comes from that very first bite.

Chomp it loud.

Chew it proud.

AWESOME!

Being able to tell my baby's cry apart from all the other crying babies at the park

....

Excruciating high-pitched wail that sounds like somebody just shot a Chihuahua?

That's the raggedy-haired two-year-old who just spun off the **merry-go-round** into a bed of milk thistles and cigarette butts.

Phlegm-filled slow-motion a-huh-huh-huh-huhhhh-huhh hhhhh?

That's the four-year-old who just got slapped after throwing sand in some kid's face in a poor attempt to draw some attention from his nanny who's been mindlessly texting beside the sandbox for an hour.

Adorable pleading a-hn-hn-hn-hn whinny?

That's my darling . . . and she needs your kid's shovel.

She's my baby and I'm her mother.

We understand each other.

So tell your little brat to raise his hands and pass it over.

Nice and slow and nobody gets hurt.

AWESOME!

—Brandis Mata, San Benito, Texas

Pulling a thick and tangly clump of hair out of the drain

Admit you like it.

We all know slippery soap suds, **rogue belly button lint**, and assorted leg hair goes down the drain easily. But **long hippie head hair** gets the bathtub traffic jamming as our tub slowly fills up till we're walking around a wading pool.

Sure, you may try to ignore it, just splashing around in soap suds up to your ankles without a care, but the truth is clogged drains aren't going anywhere, and it's time to face the truth.

It's time to get down to business.

It's time to pathetically bend your soaking wet naked body until you're face-to-face with the **Eye of Sauron** that is your bathtub drain.

Squeeze two fingers together and get digging. Slide past the oddly slippery rusted-metal sides, grab tightly onto a few rogue hairs at the top, twist a couple knot tangles around your finger, and then twirl your hand while pulling and pulling and pulling and pulling . . .

Suddenly you're a clown pulling **colorful silk hankies** out of your pocket at a magic show. How deep does it go? Does anyone know? A row of cross-legged children drop their jaws as you keep pulling and pulling and pulling and pulling until you're eventually holding something that looks like a dead vole.

AWESOME!

Seeing your parents dance

My dad might be Austin Powers.

When you open his closet it's like being transported straight into the 1960s prom scene. Dark velour suits, **purple polka-dot ties**, and frilly shirts hang beside each other like dusty friends from days gone by. "Can you spare some mothballs?" a silk shirt says to a velvet vest. "I'm not going to make it otherwise."

My dad was a high school teacher for thirty years after he came to Canada and loved chaperoning school dances and bringing my mom along. They would swirl and twirl with big smiles on their faces as they slid their **slippery shoes** across sandy gym floors deep into the high school crowd.

Like most kids, my sister and I almost always saw my parents in the context of us. Reading books before bed, steering the **bulky station wagon** to school, boiling macaroni noodles for dinner. They were always there, starring in their forever-long feature roles of Mom and Dad.

That's why it's beautiful seeing your parents dance.

When they slip into an embrace on the dance floor, they fade out of your world and into their own. **They're not parents now but just people in love.** And you get a window into what their life looks like without you, and maybe some of the reasons why you're here.

Frilly shirts, floral dresses, and velvet ties spin into **swirling twirls** that existed long before you arrived.

AWESOME!

When everything you're cooking gets done at the same time

....

Toast gets cold fast.

I'm reminded of this whenever I toss a **couple hot fried eggs** on a plate and then chomp into the cold, crumby **jam-smeared bread** lying beside them.

Hands up if you've ever watched your veggies get cold while the pot roast kept roasting, or served some **hot, piping garlic bread** while waiting thirty minutes for the lasagna to finish. Yes, eating the side dish long before the rest of the meal ranks up there in *Our Book of Annoying*, that nonexistent netherlist that also includes Painfully peeling off a Band-Aid that's stuck to your arm hair, Zippers suddenly unzipping from the bottom, and When full hugs awkwardly meet side hugs.

When microwaves ding and **ovens chime** and everything is ready all at the same time, that's a tiny little moment of bliss and a great big feeling of

AWESOME!

When the foul ball is flying towards you

....

And here's the pitch.

Bat cracks and ball smacks high into the early twilight sky. Eyeballs pop, **voices cry**, and the crowd rises as the ball starts sailing down to the stands. Drop the popcorn and smack your glove, because it's heading right for our seats.

AWESOME!

When cats do stupid things

AWESOME!

Going through a revolving door without having to push

One day my friend Matt went on a rant at the coffee shop.

"Do you realize how dangerous revolving doors are?" he began with wide popping eyes, concerned eyebrows, and a **milky foamstache** on his upper lip. "I mean, I'm surprised they're actually left unguarded in public. Don't you think it's a miracle more limbs aren't lost in those things? Crack, there goes your ankle in the door jamb. Smack, there goes your face against that impenetrable wall of glass."

He nodded his head in little bobs while staring at the napkin dispenser deep in thought.

"I think we should ban them altogether . . . while we still can."

I flashed him a thin, understanding smile while silently worrying he was becoming a bit too paranoid. What's next? Boycotting shoelaces, **avoiding escalators**, carrying a pocket thermometer to dip into drinks before sipping?

Because let's be honest: revolving doors are part of life. Due to scientific principles involving wind and air far beyond my comprehension most tall buildings make you enter through a revolving door. I think we just have to learn to enjoy the ride. Because it's sweet coasting through a revolving door . . . especially when you don't have to push:

1. **Catching a Draft.** Someone's in front of you, so their pushing gets the door moving. Just watch out, though—since they leave the door before you, it'll generally slow down fast before you get out. But be patient and let the door turn slowly. You should make it.

2. **The Invisible Force.** Here's where nobody's around but the door is spinning like mad perhaps due to some beefy strongman whipping it into a frenzy a few seconds ago while racing to catch the bus. This spinning treat resembles that big wheel on *The Price Is Right* whenever some guy from the army sends it flying. Careful getting in and then enjoy your speedy ride.

3. **The Self-Starter.** This one's like The Invisible Force, except the slow speed and deep whirring noise tells you the door is running from a power source. Incredibly unsatisfying.

4. **Sharing the Pie.** Matt's worst nightmare. Here's where you squeeze into the door right behind one of your friends. It happened fast and you didn't think it through all the way but now you're in the same little glassed-in triangle together so while they push you need to try to awkwardly speed-walk so the door doesn't keep smacking your heels.

Going through a revolving door without having to push feels like catching the **rhythm of the universe**. Entering, exiting, it doesn't matter. You surfed the wave without crumbling into a mess of dented foreheads and shattered wrists.

AWESOME!

Your birthday week

One day is not enough.

Seriously, the name birth*day* implies that annual celebrations of our lives must be squeezed into twenty-four hours. Just one day? Not nearly enough time to properly celebrate the wonder that is you!

Make sure you add in a Besties Dinner, Mandatory Fam Jam (ft. Grandma and the Cuzzies), Rogue One-on-One with That One Friend You Have From Long Ago Who None Of Your Other Friends Know And Perhaps It's Time To Cut This Thing Off But You Always Have Two Nice Dinners A Year Together And Both Come With Free Dessert, Romantic Candlelit Date Night At The Fancy Restaurant, and, of course, The Poorly Planned Boardroom Party At The Office With Melting Ice Cream Sandwiches Somebody Ran Out To Get Three Hours Ago.

AWESOME!

COMMENTS:

Annie says:

My husband started the tradition of calling our birthday weeks NAME-mas. So last month we celebrated Anniemas. It was great!

Caryn replies:

I love this!!! Our family just moved from birthday week to birthday MONTH!! My daughters both married men whose birthdays are in the same month and our philosophy is let the birthday joy last and last.

Ryan says:

One of the most amazing people I've ever known passed away a few years ago. I just got finished reading all the sweetest birthday wishes to her online. I opened this book to cheer me up after the tears only to read this page. It's like the world knew her and was touched by her kindness. RIP Emily. Happy birthday, my friend.

Pulling a shrimp out of its shell with your teeth without the tail breaking off

....

You're the master wiggler.

Nice move loosening that awkwardly curled **delicious pink meat** from the plasticky trappings of its own tail. Now you've increased your shrimp intake and can rest knowing the shrimp's life was made entirely useful.

Ashes to ashes, dust to dust, shrimp to
AWESOME!

Seeing what comes out of the garden at your new place

....

Agostino got excited.

We were hanging out in the office cafeteria one day when he started going on and on about how the previous owners of his new house had planted perennials. **"They just popped out of the ground one day,"** he said, completely astonished, eyes popping wide like a squid. "It was magic!"

He and his wife Nat bought a house and evidently gazed upon the **earthy brown patch** outside every day, enjoying the mysterious surprise of the garden and watching what bloomed out of it. I had personally never owned a house with a garden and growing up my immigrant parents always preferred the entire yard to be an untouched patch of dead grass. Very easy to maintain.

Seeing what comes out of the garden at your new place is a way humanity connects. New places usually feel empty and abandoned with rusty hangers in empty closets, **two-toned rectangles** on the carpet where the couch was, and an empty ketchup bottle and rock-hard baking soda in the fridge.

But someone was there before you and it was a home before it was your home so it's fun to take a moment to stop and think: Who used to live here? **What did they do?** Did they have kids? And a leaky basement, too?

Plants and flowers left behind form loose connections between everyone who ever lived in the same place. Popping yellow daffodils and red tulips are little notes between yesterday and tomorrow.

"Enjoy the springtime sunrise . . . and the splotch of your boots in the mud. Say hi to the hummingbirds in the flowers . . . and the ants on the peony buds."

At the end of the day we're all just tenants and if we're lucky we might have the pleasure of connection through growing maples, **shrubs**, and whatever comes out of the garden next spring.

Remember when you're moving out of your place to take your dining table, take your bed, and take your rusty drive . . . but leave something good in the garden as a little hello and high five.

AWESOME!

COMMENTS:

....

Jdurley says:

I left a perennial garden in the front yard of a house once, and the new owners covered it with sod. That was sad until next spring when I went by and saw that all my tulips had come up right through the sod! Go bulbs!

Jin says:

We were selling our house during the summer and didn't know how long it would take so we planted our usual vegetable garden. Fast forward two months to when we moved in mid-August, leaving tomatoes, peppers and carrots behind. I've always wondered if the new owners liked the little backyard bounty.

Natalie replies:

Well, I moved into a house just before harvest and, I tell you what, WE enjoyed our bounty of strawberries, peppers, squash, tomatoes, and green beans. A total bonus. I am sure your people enjoyed theirs as well!

Louise says:

We moved into our house years ago but this year, for the first time, we found a rather nondescript but pretty bush was actually a feijoa tree. We feasted on feijoas from the backyard and they tasted like strawberries, pineapple, and guava mixed together.

Kathy says:

I bought a new construction home in Houston and hired a company to take care of the landscaping. I started noticing they never cut the grass in a far corner of the yard, behind the power box, so I asked them to do it next time. The landscaping crew didn't speak English so we both used that American-translation standard: pantomiming and gesturing. After a few unfruitful minutes, one gardener took my hand and led me to the corner. There, hidden behind the power box, were the biggest, healthiest tomato plants I've ever seen. We split up the harvest. The tomatoes were unblemished, gigantic, and sooooo tasty. I guess someone must have eaten lunch during construction and a seed landed in my yard. I'm a terrible gardener and would have surely killed the plants had I tried to take care of them. Miracle Tomato Birth? AWESOME!

Seeing kids reading in the hallway

When I was in school reading was not cool.

Playing cards in the cafeteria or descending on the convenience store in droves to scam cigarettes or buy two-liter blue Slurpees, that was what lunch was all about.

I spent my lunches alone in the library with Margaret Atwood, **Alfred Lord Tennyson**, and Kurt Vonnegut. I didn't drink and was rarely invited to parties, but my memories are full from all the people I met in those library books.

Reading exploded my safe suburban world, expanded my horizons, and tenderized my teenage heart like a meat cleaver coated in MSG.

Reading sowed the seeds for me to become a writer myself.

When my old high school teacher invited me back to talk to her class about being a writer I got there and was greeted with the sight of dozens of students reading quietly in the hallways. Students with low-slung pants. Students with piercings and blue hair. Students with **short skirts and rugby shirts**. Students who spoke (and were reading in) other languages.

Science fiction and Shakespeare, poetry and fantasy, some reading solo, some reading in paperback packs.

I could hardly believe my eyes. Twenty years later, not only had reading become socially acceptable, reading had become social in and of itself.

Reading was finally cool.

I'm not sure if this is a universal transition or who we have to thank. Teachers? Parents? Harry Potter? The growing disappearance of the blue Slurpee from 7-Elevens nationwide? It doesn't matter. What matters is if the kids are reading, the kids are all right.

Reading inspires open minds, blasts off imaginations, and turns good people into even better ones. More aware, more empathetic, more understanding, less alone.

Seeing kids reading in the hallway?

AWESOME!

—Sofi Papamarko, Toronto, Ontario

That little hole at the top of your sink that prevents it from overflowing

Let's face it.

We're all cranking taps with no idea when our reckless shaving or **face-washing shenanigans** might flood our bathroom floors.

Thanks for watching our backs, hole.

AWESOME!

Tearing off a piece of plastic wrap that doesn't immediately get stuck to itself

Plastic wrap is trouble.

When you're peeling a new sheet from the flimsy cardboard box, I've got just two words for you: **Watch out!**

Somehow this product is actually sold without labels warning us that most of the time it's just going to get stuck to itself. Does this happen to you? You try peeling it off but while doing that the wrap sticks to *other* parts of the wrap and then while trying to peel it apart you just get more stuck together and it very quickly dawns on you that, yet again, the plastic wrap has punched you out. With your blood boiling you roll it into a squishy, unsatisfying ball and pitch it into the trash.

Ding ding ding!

Crack your neck and get your dukes up because it's time for round two. Sweat blurs your vision but you kick your stool away from the corner of the mat before steadying your menacing gaze on that thin cardboard box.

Do a few little jumps left, few little jumps right, pop a couple quick **air jabs**, and look to the crowd for energy as you mime a big uppercut. Now that you're revved up it's time to quickly run up and grab the box, squeeze its top tightly in a highly illegal choke hold, and then, as the crowd roars, just rake your hands from top to bottom and quickly pull the wrap over the tiny ridge of metal teeth.

You did it!

Drop the box on the mat and hold the beautifully smooth sheet of plastic wrap up in the air. Tears fall down your **bloody and black-eyed face** as the crowd goes wild and the ringside announcers scream.

Now fly like a butterfly to the counter and drape it over that bowl of potato salad.

AWESOME!

Socks as an expression of personality

....

Tightly coiffed haircut. Thick black glasses. Dark blue jeans and striped shirt open at the collar. Blazer on the back of the chair at the vegan restaurant. And then they stand up and you see them.

Neon socks with fireworks.

Don't just sit there.

Say hi.

AWESOME!

Making it through airport security without any beeps

AWESOME!

When you get in the car and notice someone filled up the tank

Thank you, Car Partner.

You left us a little surprise in the driveway and now we're as far as possible from needing to make an annoying pump run while we're already late for work.

Also, it's always hilarious when you see that little orange arm nudging itself up **even higher than Full** on the gas gauge. It's like it's winking at you saying, "Okay, I was lying about the size of my tank but now I really can't take another drop."

Also applies to discovering someone greased your bike chain, plugged your electric car in overnight, or wiped all the snow off your helicopter blades.

AWESOME!

Watching your favorite movie with someone who hasn't seen it before

···

Do you remember the first time?

Were you in **red plushy seats** at the movie theater, curled up under a pile of basement blankets, or maybe by yourself on a long flight?

I was in college sitting on a dusty, moth-eaten, floral-patterned couch in a room with thick wainscoting and 14-foot-ceilings with an actual bat living in the corner. That's where I first saw *Annie Hall* and felt its snappy dialogue, twisting plotlines, and heart-wrenching story suck me in like a vacuum.

Since then I have taken great pleasure in giving friends their first *Annie Hall* showing. After they tell me they haven't seen it I do that really annoying thing where I insist they have to, but perhaps slightly less annoying thing of actually scheduling it.

Reserving a special night is important.

I prepare by dimming the lights, **making popcorn**, and whipping their cell phone down the basement stairs.

Yes, there's a lot of buildup, pressure, and expectations. But when it delivers, that's the fun.

Seeing their eyes flicker, **laughing at the same jokes**, and hearing them guess what might happen next makes it feel like sharing part of your heart.

AWESOME!

When you get a package delivered while you're on a call and the dog doesn't bark

....

My friend Scott had a Jack Russell terrier.

Whenever I rang his doorbell that small white dog with brown spots came flying down the front hall **yipping his brains out** while racing towards the glass door. And what did he do when he got close to the door? Suddenly stop on the slippery mat? No, he jumped three feet in the air and slammed his entire body against the glass.

Did he then collapse into a crumpled whimper? Oh no! He just got up and did it again. And again. **And again.** Until Scott carefully opened the door to let me squeeze in, at which point the dog redirected his leaping onto me.

Dog brains clearly haven't evolved proper responses to doorbells. Maybe they think a gun is going off on a hunting plain or some trumpeting animal is preparing to attack. It might take centuries to develop a chill response to the dinging delivery guy.

Congratulations if your dog has figured it out.

That's one highly evolved mutt.

AWESOME!

Going really fast over speed bumps at the back of a school bus

....

The back of the school bus is a **strange seatbeltless land** far from teachers, parents, and watching eyes. Slide on the slippery vinyl seats, wipe your nose on your sleeve, and laugh out loud with your eight-year-old pals as you bounce home from school.

When the school bus zooms over a huge bump, there's suddenly a blurry scene of flying elbow-scabbed arms and grass-stained knees. Butts fly off seats, faces smack windows, and, if you're lucky, some kid **sucking on a juice box** might even go rolling right down the aisle.

You keep your loopy roller coasters and your fancy water slides.

We'll take smacking speed bumps on our wild school bus rides.

AWESOME!

Smelling someone barbecuing over your backyard fence

AWESOME!

Realizing you accomplished nothing so far today so deciding to spend a few minutes cleaning up your computer desktop and calling that a win

It feels like anything is possible in the morning.

Sit down for work and eyeball a couple scattered afternoon meetings, make a mental list of priorities, and take a deep breath before diving in.

But wait, before you do, better check your inbox and—oh look—a dozen emails clamoring for your attention. **One from the boss!** Better answer that first. While collecting your thoughts a few more drop in. Couple texts. A quick request. And now here come the meetings.

Five minutes before quitting time you realize you have done exactly nothing you planned to do. You sat through meetings, answered emails, but crossed nothing off your list.

Do you go pick up the kids feeling like a failure?

No!

It's time to invest a furious three minutes cleaning up your computer desktop by throwing files in folders, **deleting screenshots**, and emptying the trash.

Success!

You have turned the day from waste to win.
Swirl out of your chair because it's time to head home.
Peel your socks off, put your feet up, and crack a cold one.
We'll see you again tomorrow.
AWESOME!

When your parent brings you back a gift from their business trip

It's a tiny paper-wrapped bar of soap, mesh bag of chocolate coins, teddy bear dressed as a Buckingham Palace guard, **little foam shoe shiner thing**, extra-clicky clicky pen, tiny bottle of maple syrup, matches from a really good restaurant, bedroom door nameplate with slightly incorrect spelling of your name, stack of Niagara Falls postcards, **tiny room service ketchup bottle**, extra-extra-large T-shirt with "The Year Of YOU!" plastered across the chest, or one of those rocks cut in half and all purple and sparkly in the middle.

How did you know?

AWESOME!

"Here's another thing I find awesome: Finding pistachios that have fallen out of their shell in the bag. When I have the munchies, not much beats a salty handful of pistachios. But when I'm rooting through the bag, I find that not all of them are created equal. In fact, there are four kinds of pistachios offering varying degrees of difficulty:

1. **Shell completely closed.** These ones are a lost cause, so I always toss them right back into the bag. Maybe some other ambitious soul will try to crack them open, but more likely, they're gonna find a home in the trash bin.
2. **Shell just a tiny sliver open.** These ones are tricky but stand a chance of being eaten. Whether I throw these ones back in the bag or not will depend on how long my thumbnails are and how hungry I am.
3. **Shell open wide.** These are great. When I'm peckish, I can open these ones in rapid-fire succession without a hitch. Before I've even realized it, because I'm watching shark videos online, I've ripped through like three handfuls.
4. **The ones that have fallen out of their shells.** The crown jewels of pistachios. No fuss. No work. Just

AWESOME!"

—Adrian Fiorino

When that old restaurant you love but haven't been to in twenty years is still there when you go back

....

There was something about Za Master.

A hole-in-the-wall place with long lines out the door and down the street after the bars emptied, with pizza slices sitting in a **glassed-in cube** under a heating light on a faded orange counter, offering your choice of cheese, pepperoni, and all-dressed.

Poutine was packed into Styrofoam drums with a layer of crispy fries, steaming gravy, and squeaky cheese curds topped with . . . another layer of crispy fries, thick gravy, and squeaky cheese curds.

Grilled chicken pitas were slathered in creamy tzatziki before dill pickles, grilled onions, banana peppers, green olives, pineapple, and a big handful of shredded iceberg lettuce was rolled in.

The place was run by Sal, an old Italian guy in a dirty apron who wore dark glasses and had a thick white ribbon rivering through his frizzy black hair. As if to cement his reputation as a local icon, the walls of Za Master were covered entirely in graffiti movie posters starring Sal. **MEN IN SAL** featured Sal in a dark suit and shades holding an assorted pita in place of a machine gun. SALBO had Sal in place of Sylvester Stallone, and TERMINATOR SAL featured a half Sal/half cyborg staring at you with his glowing red eye as you tipsily slid through dirty slush on your way to the counter at two in the morning.

A short archway to the left of the cash led from the fluorescently lit Za Master into the darker Za Bar next door. And if it was midnight on a Tuesday and everyone was really into the card game in the common room, you could skip the freezing walk up to Princess Street, call in an order, and within an hour a **shivering skinny guy** with a wispy mustache smoking a cigarette would be banging on the glass door in the front of your residence holding a paper bag.

Za Master was one of my favorite restaurants in Kingston.

Sadly, in my third year living there it was front-page news that Za Master was suddenly stripped of their liquor license after apparently serving underage students in Za Bar. The restaurant shuttered. We never saw Sal again. I missed Za Master the next two years I lived there and still miss it every time I drive by where it used to be . . .

  . . . used to be

    . . . used to be

      . . . used to be

There was something about Wok-In.

A hole-in-the-wall Cambodian, Thai, and Vietnamese place wedged between a night club and a methadone clinic with a five-foot-tall couple from Phnom Penh behind the cash. They parked their old black **Mercedes-Benz** outside the restaurant and sometimes would be inside loudly cussing the parking guy after getting a ticket.

That was the only time you would hear him speak because he usually just nodded gently while taking your order. She was always speaking Cambodian nonstop behind him—wedging tomatoes, **washing cilantro**, chopping chilis. The phone was always ringing in the background because they couldn't accept takeout orders when the five lacquered wooden booths out front were full.

You would order a #1 or #7 or #13 and then grab a giant Brita water filter pitcher from the fridge and a couple Styrofoam cups from the counter. Twenty minutes later she would carry your deep ceramic plate to you (mutely with no eye contact) on an orange cafeteria tray alongside thin white napkins, a metal fork and knife, and a pair of wooden chopsticks in a paper sleeve. Creamy red curry or thick chili-filled broth filled the plate and as you ate the dish revealed **dense maroon swirls** underneath. The bathroom was past a pile of paper towels, through a sliding accordion door, inside a room with a short toilet, thick toilet paper, good soap, and a tarnished gold statue on the tiny trapezoidal sink.

Wok-In was one of my favorite restaurants in Kingston.

Wok-In *is* one of my favorite restaurants in Kingston.

Over the past twenty years, I have driven through Kingston many times, and as long as it's not a Sunday, a Monday, before 11:30 a.m., between 2:00 and 4:30 p.m., or after 9:00 p.m., I always swing by for a #13. It's as delicious as I remember every time and I enjoy revisiting the **invisible shadow** of myself when I'm sitting there. Stomping snow off my boots with my first girlfriend, slow-slurping steaming broth on cold days, it's always a gift reliving the memories in the same place.

The couple hunches a bit more and their hair is getting gray but there is deep joy sharing connection and deep joy sharing the day.

AWESOME!

The first day of the year you get to wear shorts

AWESOME!

When you're sleeping and the sounds around you meld into your dreams

....

Snores are steam trains, clock radios are car alarms, and the neighbor building a deck outside is someone knocking urgently at your front door.

When the sounds around your sleeping self magically morph into **new stories in new worlds** it's a reminder that the wild horses of your mind can take you far, far away.

Eyes closed, **fingers limp**, breathing as deep as rolling ocean waves . . . and then lightning crashes, faces flashes, and you float deeper into alternate lives in that endlessly splintering multiverse of thoughts.

When you wake up, make sure to keep bubbling with big ideas, **race those winning races**, and keep your heart beating fast.

Being a dreamer is great fun.

Being a dreamer?

Truly

AWESOME!

Slipping in the tub but catching yourself at the last second

....

You almost took a **nude and soapy tumble** into that slippery ceramic tub.

But then you didn't.

AWESOME!

A la moding anything

....

Leslie and I were walking around a new neighborhood one night a couple years into our relationship when we strolled past a giant restaurant window with a tall guy standing inside wearing a paper hat swiping a **tiny windshield wiper** across a hot black circle on the counter in front of him.

We watched mesmerized as the creamy batter he was swirling and quickly flipping cooked into thin spongy crepes with crispy edges. He peeled the crepe off the circle and gave us a wink that said, "We both know you're coming in to buy one of these right now."

I am a huge fan of Willy Wonka factory–type cooking experiences and as we stepped in the door my mind flashbacked to watching tiny donuts float down **Hot Oil Rapids** at the supermarket when I was a kid, seeing fresh waffle cones pressed and rolled at a local ice cream shop, and, of course, the trauma of my poor brother Augustus falling into a chocolate river.

After Leslie and I ordered a crepe, the man in the paper hat sprinkled it with chopped strawberries, doused it in chocolate sauce, and then paused for a second to ask us the big question:

"Would you like ice cream on top?"

I don't know my local bylaws very well but I'm sure there's one stipulating that anyone ordering a giant crepe covered in strawberries and chocolate sauce on a Friday night must say yes to ice cream. You don't want to get tossed in the slammer for screwing up dessert.

Moments later we were scarfing down the sweet, creamy, burning-hot, freezing-cold crepe and it got me thinking that adding a scoop of ice cream—or a la moding anything—just makes food much better.

Shall we examine the hypothesis?

1. **Pie.** Let's start with a classic. Apple pie without ice cream is a gummy and crumbling mess. The melting scoop of vanilla provides texture and balance while also testing your molar fillings with shocking hot and cold sensitivity.

2. **A glass of Coke.** Turn a boring cup of fizz into an ice cream float in just one scoop. Time is a key ingredient here. Do you spoon the melting pools of vanilla while alternating sips of cold cola or wait a minute before stirring the whole thing together into endless creamy bubbliness?

3. **Waffles.** Let's head back into the Doughy Family Tree for a moment. You've got Momma Pancake, Crazy Uncle Funnel Cake, and, of course, Cousin Waffle. Make sure to spread the melting ice cream into every possible little square. Glug maple syrup over the whole thing before enjoying a somewhat mathematical Grid of Deliciosity. Bonus points if you pull this off at breakfast.

4. **Something weird that none of us have tried before but that's probably delicious.** Do you add ice cream to

smoothies, brownies, or pineapple pizza? We're not judging. We're just trying to learn. The point is that the world of a la moding has no limits and sometimes off-the-wall ideas go a long way. You can a la mode a bowl of pain au chocolats for a classic French brunch or maybe a la mode some chicken fried rice for a truly authentic Asian experience.

5. **Birthday cake.** The flavor and texture of warm-and-spongy-icing-smeared birthday cake mouth-merging with freezing-cold melty vanilla ice cream is an unparalleled experience. You just hit À la Mode Nirvana. And yes, when you reach that level you're ready for the accent.

Adding a scoop of ice cream really does make everything better.

So let's stop and sing it loud!
For all the boys and girls!
Let's hold each others' hands!
And à la mode the world!

AWESOME!

When a butterfly lands on that flower right on the edge of the trail you're hiking

It's a beautiful nature cameo.
AWESOME!

Thinking

....

"How often do you think?"

I remember my eleventh grade English teacher interrupting class one day with that question. We'd been busy having stapler fights, **passing notes**, and half-heartedly working on book reports about *Lord of the Flies* when he just sort of paused to challenge us a bit.

"I mean how often do you actually sit back and think?" he asked. The room was silent. "I ask you because you're really lucky you have the ability to think. You should remember that."

He paused for a few seconds and looked at us and we paused for a few seconds and looked back. Whatever profound conversation he was trying to have quickly stutter-stopped so we shrugged and began chatting again. Some doodled, some leaned back in chairs, and a couple kids in the corner **rubbed glue sticks** on each other's sweatshirts.

It was a long time ago.

I didn't think about it for years.

But then one day I was finishing up a speech and was gathering my things and stepping off the stage when a man rushed up to me.

"Hey, I got one for the next book," he started in urgently. I looked up to see wild eyes darting through **thick glasses**, a weathered face, and black shaggy hair rolling down past his neck.

"Thinking."

He stared at me for a reaction.

"Thinking," he said again.

"Yeah, that's true," I said. "Thinking is . . . pretty important."

"No, no, you don't understand," he said sharply, **slightly spitting**, his hands shaking urgently. "I mean just remembering you have the ability to think. I was in a big car accident last year and my head got hit pretty bad. I spent a year in a coma in the hospital . . . and I couldn't think. I couldn't process thoughts. I knew I was alive but I wasn't able to have thoughts connect in my brain."

I must have looked stunned, but he kept going.

"I got out of the hospital a few weeks ago and I'm doing great. I can think again and it's such a gift. We aren't always able to think . . . but if you can, if you can put things together, if you can figure things out, then you're lucky. I missed a year of my life because I couldn't think. I will never take it for granted again."

My mind flashbacked to that **eleventh grade classroom** with my teacher failing to get our attention. We didn't understand his point then. How could we? When you've always thought, when you can always think, it's hard seeing you have that ability and hard to imagine not being able to.

So go ahead and think right now about whatever you want to think. Whatever you want! No shame. No guilt. No judgment. You are thinking. It's okay to think what you're thinking. It's beautiful to be able to do that.

Let's stop for a moment to remember the liberating freedom in that raw ability.

Let's stop to remember it's
AWESOME!

Trying on the most ridiculous sunglasses you can find at the store

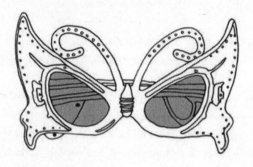

AWESOME!

Giving thanks

....

It's a two-step process (with a few rules) that will change your life, and will change the life of someone else, every day.

Step 1: Get a stack of 3 × 5 index cards. They could have lines. They could be totally blank. They could be pink. It's up to you.

Step 2: At least once a day, write a note on one of these cards. An unsigned, specific, generous, and true note thanking someone. It could be something you leave with the tip at a coffee shop where the server smiled, or it could be something you mail to someone you've worked with for years.

The only rules are:

- You're not allowed to let anyone else see you delivering the note, and if you give it to someone in person, you should try to leave before they read it.
- It has to be true.
- There needs to be no upside for you. If you get a free lunch out of it, it doesn't count.

AWESOME!

—*Seth Godin, Hastings-on-Hudson, New York*

Twisting the lid off the jar after nobody else could

I used to hang out at Jean's place.

Back when I was in second grade and my sister Nina was in kindergarten we spent our lunchtimes and after-schools at a DIY day care run by a thin, leathery woman named Jean. She wore her dark, frizzy hair up in a denim tie and chain-smoked upstairs at her kitchen table, but to us her home was a dark underground playground of plastic toys and *Thundercats* reruns and we spent hours and hours there for years and years.

At lunchtime the seven or eight kids she looked after crowded around a wobbly plastic table to dive into grilled Cheez Whiz on buttery white bread, **mayo-drenched tuna casseroles**, or bologna and processed cheese sandwiches cut into triangles. Jean always capped each meal by pouring a jar of apple sauce, **syrupy peach slices**, or goopy fruit salad with neon-red cherries into little bowls for us.

I remember watching skinny Jean try to open those fat jars. She'd be huffing and puffing till we thought she'd fall over. Sometimes she'd hold the jar under hot water, other times she'd twist with a dishcloth, and then there was my favorite—the spectacularly loud bang-and-clang-the-lid-with-a-wooden-spoon move, which we always expected would result in our servings of pear halves sprinkled with shattered glass.

Poor Jean was surrounded by a weak and wide-eyed army of tiny hands, **spaghetti-noodle arms**, and saggy triceps. We couldn't help much, but after watching her suffer for years we pledged to always help others open tough-to-open jars whenever life gave us the chance.

Twisting a lid off the jar after nobody else could fills you with **Superhero Pride**. Suddenly you're Wonder Woman, Mr. Universe, or a big-handed Hulk, beaming with a big smile as you hand back that freshly popped jar of

AWESOME!

A tiny bird singing its heart out alone on a power wire in an empty parking lot

Orange skies burn as winds whisper for your chilly walk home. Sun kisses the horizon and **dogs bark behind backyard fences** as your hair blows sideways in the suddenly sharp breeze. You squint into the wind and slide your hands into thin pockets as you sniff up smoky sweet smells of garage barbecues, **dusty furnace fumes**, and dead leaves.

You spot a tiny bird tightly gripping a black power wire above the parking lot in front of the old gas station. Against dry leaves blowing and that whistling wind the bird has its chest up, its eyes closed, and is just singing singing singing singing singing.

No one else sees it. No one else hears it.

Seasons changing, **life rearranging**, and we all just keep singing on . . .

AWESOME!

Peeling a hard-boiled egg and getting a big chunk of shell off all at once

Flick.

Operating room lights snap on.

Camera bangs through flipping plastic doors and into a room with bright overhead lights and a half dozen nurses in baby-blue scrubs and face shields all staring at you expectantly. You look at the operating table and yes, there it is—a large soft and smooth brown curve. Rap it with your knuckle. As you expected. Hard as bone.

Before you begin it's time to glance up at the gallery of surgeons holding pens and notepads waiting on every move.

You smile softly, nod back down at the nurses, and then bring your fist to its highest point before suddenly swinging it down for a deafening crack. Rivers splinter in all directions and you start slowly picking off a **few small triangles** to get started. Then it happens. The moment everybody has been waiting for. You spy a big jagged piece on the top left side. It looks like you can maybe slide your latex-gloved finger in there. You look at the head nurse. He nods. You nod.

You take a deep breath.

You nod gently three times.

You get one finger slightly underneath while the other hand holds a tight grip on a long straight edge.

You tighten your stomach, lift, and . . . the entire top of the shell comes off!

You smile at them all, gently wave to the applause, and then, in a shocking finale, just sprinkle a bit of salt on the body, bare your teeth, and dive in face-first.

AWESOME!

Racing outside to put your garbage out but missing the truck so then just casually walking across the street in your robe and leaving it in with your neighbors' bins because theirs gets picked up later

....

Every morning I wake up with a simple goal:

Keep wearing my robe as long as possible.

Are you with me on this? I know I'm not alone. Good days net me an hour or two. On the weekend I might make it to lunch.

Robe and slippers are my perfect transition between "heavy sheets and blankets" to "sweatpants and a hoodie." I think it's because the robe feels like I'm taking my bed with me as I begin my day. No changing time, strong shin coverage, legs comfortably sashaying as I stumble around the kitchen looking for the frying pan.

Once a week my comfy robe morning is jarringly interrupted by a sudden realization that today is garbage day and I haven't put the bins out. I drop everything and dangerously attempt the **Barefooted Bed-Headed Blowing-Robe Scramble** of wheeling my bins to the curb before the truck comes. I put everything I have into pulling it off, which is why it always feels heartbreaking to discover the truck already went past.

Now I am left with two choices:

1. **Pull my bins back.** Pathetically slump my shoulders, bow my head, and wheel my stuffed bins back to the side of my house. This is the official option approved by the city. Garbage didn't make it? That's on you. But it results in a week of endlessly squishing stinky bags and fending off raccoons while being harshly reminded of the garbage gaffe.

2. **Put my bins somewhere else.** This is the confident power play. If I'm lucky and my neighbors across the street haven't had their garbage picked up yet I look left, look right, and nonchalantly strut over in bare feet and blowing robe before casually mixing my bins in with theirs. Now when the garbage truck comes back up the street later my garbage will get tossed in the truck.

I came, I walked, I threw out the garbage.
That easily earns me another hour of Robe Time.
AWESOME!

Getting a good locker in high school

Scott got screwed.

Back in ninth grade my friend Scott was assigned a **locker buddy** named Kyle, who played trumpet in the school band.

They shared a thin locker down a dark and dusty hallway outside the Boy's Changeroom. Not only was it a five-minute hike from any of our classes but it had the side benefit of permanently smelling like 16-year-old armpit.

Scott gave Kyle the top shelf so he was stuck on his knees every morning stuffing his **winter jacket, books, and boots** onto the rusty floor of the thing. I have a painfully vivid memory of watching Kyle's brick-like trumpet case majestically soar from the top shelf and slam right into Scott's forehead.

You could say he had a bad locker.

Getting a good locker in high school makes all the difference.

You need a convenient spot to grab your books when you're running late, easy access to the bathroom and cafeteria, and a good **Locker Neighborhood** near all your friends.

Flying trumpet cases to the forehead should be avoided wherever possible.

AWESOME!

That one pair of pants that makes your ass look great

....

You've checked from every angle.
   You've checked in every light.
   You've checked the storefront window.
   That ass looks dynamite.
   AWESOME!

Texting your husband to do something when he's upstairs and you're downstairs

....

Did you see the movie *Elf*?

I loved that scene where a mailroom guy in the basement of the **Empire State Building** puts some papers in one of those tennis ball containers and zips it up to the seventy-seventh floor through that system of windy vacuum tubes snaking inside the building walls.

I remember seeing that in office buildings when I was a kid and thinking yes, yes, this technology is going to take off. Sure, we may need to mildly renovate every tall building in the world back to the studs but, you know, wouldn't it be worth it to fire an invoice up to **Sonia in Accounting** without taking the stairs?

Well, my dream never quite came true but I do think of that distant fantasy whenever my wife Leslie texts me from the kitchen asking if I can bring down the basket of dirty laundry.

The future has arrived.

AWESOME!

Really, really tall people

They're tall and there's nothing they can do about it except learn to live with their crazy tallness. For this reason, we respect them and think they're cool.

If you're really, really tall, you feel it because this is your life:

- **Everyone hates you at movies and concerts.** Sure, you get a decent sight line, but at what price? Everybody resents you and you have to put up with constant shuffling and people saying things like "Oh great, I'm stuck behind Stilts here."
- **Guaranteed back pain.** Duck into a car and lean over to tie your shoes enough times and you'll eventually score some sharp, shooting pains in that lower lumbar.
- **Hard to date people.** Well, not hard, but complicated. I mean, would you date someone really, really tall? If not, you see the problem here.
- **You are forced to play basketball.** Doesn't matter if you like it, doesn't matter if you don't—you just have to play. Also, if you're no good you'll never hear the end of it and if you are good people will say it's just because you're really, really tall.
- **People always want you to get stuff from the top shelf.** And guess what else comes with that giant soup pot nobody's used in two years? A faceful of dust, that's what. Hope you're not allergic.

- **You're always hitting your head on everything.** If you're really, really tall, you know what I mean, because your skull is full of spider cracks from chandeliers, basement stairwells, and airplane overhead bins.
- **Life is more expensive.** King-sized mattresses, raisable desks, and paying extra for Emergency Exit aisles on airplanes adds up.

It's a tough life.

So next time you see a really, really tall person, break out the empathy. Remember: they're tall and there's nothing they can do except learn to live with their **crazy tallness**. In this upside-down and inside-out world, that's worth something.

Throw them a smile and a nod, a leaping high five, or just some quiet respect.

AWESOME!

COMMENTS:

....

Audrey says:

I am 6'1". I love this page. It's nice to hear some empathy. I can only tell people I don't like basketball so many times.

> *Gina replies:*
>
> I'm 6'1", too. I get asked the basketball question a lot. A friend told me to ask back if they play miniature golf!
>
> *Hayley replies:*
>
> I'm 6'3" and I just love to wear heels!

Freddo says:

I once stood directly behind 7'7" former NBA player Manute Bol in the airport circuity line at O'Hare in Chicago. He was walking with a cane that was, no joke, as tall as my wife. Plus, even though only about 20% of the airport knew him from his playing days, 100% of the people were staring at him. Made you really feel for the guy. Since I've been average height all my life, I decided to marry into a really short family, and now I feel really tall by comparison. Take that, average-height genes!

Tom says:

I'm 6'8" but when asked I say I'm 5'20".

> *Penny replies:*
>
> Centimeters works, too! That really throws them. I say 190 centimeters.

Brice says:

I am 6'7" and don't forget if you don't play basketball people may get mad for wasting your tallness. I may pursue a literary career or one in the ministry, thank you very much!

Ada says:

I am 5'7" and my boyfriend is 6'10". We have figured out so many ways to kiss without me standing on my tippy toes with him slouching down. I stand on the driver's side door thing, I sit on top of my car, he sits on the hood, or we both sit down! But I love wearing heels and getting the extra legroom seats when we travel together.

Showing old people how to do something on their phone

It makes you feel like a genius.
AWESOME!

Singing in the car on the way home from the concert

··

Stamped hands and **plastic wristbands** cover the sweaty crowd as the houselights flicker on at the end of the show.

Everyone **bumps and grinds** to the bathroom as eyes adjust and ears pop. Minutes later you pile into the car with your friends and buckle up for a traffic-jammy trip out of the parking lot, way down the highway, and finally home to bed.

Killing an hour on your way home from a concert is a piece of cake, though. Just roll down those windows, pump those fists, honk that horn, and get ready to scrape that scratchy throat.

Time for the loud, screechy sing-a-long of Tonight's Greatest Hits.

AWESOME!

Getting dressed out of the laundry basket

....

Hands up if you've ever been a bachelor.

Do you know the **lazy-boned joy** of sleeping in a bed half-covered in clothes? The amazing innovation of eating breakfast **over the sink** to avoid using one of your three plates? And, of course, the time-saving brilliance of getting dressed straight out of the laundry basket?

You know how it goes: Alarm clock buzzes and you're suddenly grog-sliding around your cramped apartment with one eye open. After opening your dresser drawers and finding them empty, your eyes dart around until you spy the pile of clean clothes in the laundry basket in the corner. Now it's time to fish through the static-peeling pile until you find socks, underwear, and a hoodie to go with the stained sweatpants lying beside your bed.

Folding underwear, ironing shirts, rolling up socks?

No thanks.

We'll fill our days with five extra minutes of AWESOME!

Redoing a high five with a friend to get a better smack

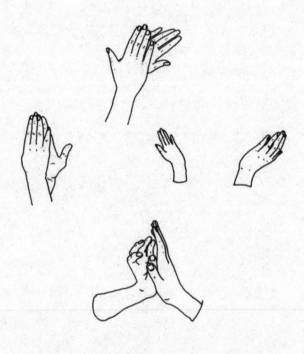

AWESOME!

"i want to add a few more:

    -that full body stretch in the morning before you have your coffee and shower

    -reading a newspaper when the center pages are still warm from the press

    -when you get winter tires on your car and just the thought of having them makes you feel like good now i won't end up in a ditch like i did last year because of those cheap ass tires i was using which were great for back east but a really bad idea in the prairies because of all the unplowed streets and not having control over your car and always thinking you're gonna hit somebody shoveling right on the side of the road

    -the feeling just before and after eating that sour candy that you just know is going to hit you right below the ears and in the back of your throat

    -going to the hair salon and having your hair washed right before it's cut and the hair stylist gives you one of those head massages where it feels like a full body massage because she rubs your head and your neck and your forehead and honestly i call it having my ears cleaned cause i hear so much better after ... see you at 345 after work janice!!!!!!!!"

—hélène

Backing away from the crib like a ninja

....

It's a high-pressure scene.

Your baby has fallen asleep in her crib and now it's time for your big getaway. This is the scene after Bond secures the hard drive but still has to tiptoe across that ledge to get the security cameras, feed a few guard dogs, and steal the bad guy's Ferrari.

Before making your move: freeze for a moment to process Current Sleep Status. Do we have completely shut eyes and deep, nearly silent baby breathing? Or are the whites of the eyes visible through slits like she's suddenly The Undertaker? Any bursts of random sleep-crying? Babbling?

Depending on how she's sleeping you need to pick a Stealth Mode and start moving:

Stealth Mode 1: She's dozing deeply so as long as you don't trip on any dolls or squeak toys on the way out, you're fine. Of course, it's still important to avoid that long-memorized pattern of creaky floorboards. You can walk out quickly. Just no false moves.

Stealth Mode 2: The slumber isn't well-settled so normal human steps pose a risk. You need to take one step, pause for ten seconds, take a second step, pause for ten seconds, and so on. Halfway to the door you may hear a sigh that will freeze you in your tracks, but you can't even risk twisting around because a simple back crack will give you away. Take a slow breath and settle into Warrior Pose. You could be here a while.

Stealth Mode 3: She's still got one eye open and is finger-playing with her blanket but the fourth quarter of the game is about to start so you have to risk it. Your odds of a successful exit here is less than 10%. Even normal human breathing poses a risk. Picture yourself high up in the darkening forest canopy as the sun dips down. Drop down silently and land on your knees. Take a very long deep breath and begin slow-crawling for the door. Search the floor for mines with your knees before putting weight down anywhere. Keep your head sideways the whole time with an eye fixed on the baby, spying for any sudden moves. If there is a shuffle you must immediately drop to your stomach and do not, whatever you do, do not move a muscle. After holding your breath for a minute slowly exhale and then reach your baby finger forward to quietly pull open the door a bit and then shimmy closer to it. When you're finally within door-opening distance quickly perform a silent backflip-somersault to your feet and then flash open and close the door and slip out before any hallway light blinds her.

Wait outside the door a minute and make sure to wildly pop your eyes open and shake your head vigorously with a big finger over your mouth if your partner walks by. While he stares at you with a weird look carrying a laundry basket do not change your straight face. Just look left, look right, and race down the stairs into the forest blackness.

You are a true parenting ninja.

Now flip on the game.

AWESOME!

—*Brian Shaw, New York City*

Using milk instead of water

What's up, instructions?

Why are you recommending water in our pancakes, **hot chocolate**, and Jell-O pudding? Why are you trying to blandify our oatmeal, brownies, and mushroom soup?

Look, we're sorry, but there's a new cook in the kitchen and things are going to be a lit-tle different around here from now on. Yes, we're talking creamier hot chocolate, **puffier pancakes**, and brownies that will make tears of joy spray out your eyes like a sprinkler.

We're talking about using milk instead of water, baby.

AWESOME!

Your saliva

....

Entertaining kids is cheap.

Forget big-screen TVs, Super Bowl tickets, or schlepping them to some thatched hut on stilts in the middle of the ocean. No, you can ditch those in favor of an afternoon playing Tag in the backyard, pillow fighting in the bedroom, or trying to keep a balloon up in the air for as long as possible.

It seems like a lot of kids figure out how to entertain themselves on the cheap, too. I don't mean grabbing for the phone or video game controller, either. I mean those weird little head games or **counting games** or pattern games you sometimes see little kids playing. Do you know what I mean? I'm sure these days it's referred to as Acute Juvenile-Onset Countosis—AJOC—or something, but it used to be that little kids were just a little, you know, strange.

I think strangeness is part of the patchwork field from which creativity and ideas grow. My strange six-year-old self loved spinning into incredible states of dizziness, playing with **cherry stems** in my mouth for hours, and sitting in the backseat of the family station wagon on the highway and gently touching my fingertips together while counting up by tens while *also* trying to subtract from my rapidly increasing number the cars driving past us in the other direction with the goal of trying to always stay on *this* side of zero.

Like I said, the games were strange but you have to remember the fate of the world was at stake.

I'm pretty sure my favorite **Weird Kid Game** was when I would look down at my shoes and slowly let a thin strand of saliva slide slowly from my mouth—as low as it would go, as slow as it would go. And only when that spiderlike string seemed at its breaking point would I suddenly suck real fast, slurping air-chilled spit into my waiting mouth in one soaring, majestic move. Cirque du Soleil, if you're reading this, give me a call.

Now, back then I would pull off my famous **Saliva Slurp-Back** without realizing the sheer power of the stuff. Saliva has serious superpowers. Do you remember when we talked about Your Colon? Well, now it's time to examine what's happening at the other end. Your saliva's superpowers include:

1. **Wets and whets.** Saliva secretes out of a few little glands in your mouth at a rate of around one to two *liters* a day. Endless saliva tides rise and help moisten crunchy granola, seedy sandwich crusts, and crispy crackers in order to help them slide down the dark cavern of your throat. First benefit? Food lube.

2. **Get your taste on.** Now, did you know that for all its powers your poor tongue can't taste a thing when it's dry? It's true! Sorry if this feels like finding out Superman can't fly when it's cold out but a dry tongue really does equal endlessly tasteless food. So it's time to start thinking of saliva as the salt of your mouth. There it is, quietly keeping everything tasty, flavorful, and delicious.

3. **Break it down.** Even though more than 99.5% of your saliva is water, there's a lot going on in that other 0.5%. I'm talking about electrolytes, mucus, antibacterial compounds, and enzymes. What's all that for? Swimming into your food and starting to wrestle it into bits, that's the first thing. Tearing starch and fat molecules to smithereens and giving them the what's what. Yes, your esophagus, stomach, intestines, and colon are part of this dream team but saliva is first on the job.

4. **Mouthguards.** There's no nice way to say this so I'm just going to say it: You are a messy eater. Shawarma or no shawarma, just look at all those bits of meat wedged in your teeth and the Corn Pops filling your molars. Thank goodness saliva flushes your mouth all day to keep your disgusting mouth in pretty good shape and prevent tooth decay.

You won't hear saliva tooting its own horn or singing its own praises. It's a real team player who knows its job is to fight on the front lines of your digestive system. Comes early, stays late, working hard till the very end.

So today let's say thank you, saliva.

For all you do.

AWESOME!

Waiters and waitresses who know the menu really well

....

I think I'd make a bad waiter.

Balancing trays of dirty glasses, sliding on slick kitchen floors, and rushing for refills is beyond my abilities. It's a tough job beyond a lot of people's abilities, like for instance:

1. **No-Notepad Nancy.** This is the gal who listens to everyone's order without writing anything down. No pen, no notes, nothing. At first you're impressed but the wow factor disappears half an hour later when all the meals come out wrong.
2. **Disappearing Danesh.** He's great during drinks and dinner, but after that—poof!—it's like a cloud of smoke explodes and he just vanishes. Dirty dishes linger and you're stuck wandering around aimlessly shoulder-tapping anyone in an apron asking for the bill.
3. **Spilly Sook-Yin.** Watch out for that matzo ball soup! Sook-Yin is a bit of a klutz so get ready for wet tablecloths, skidding fries, and glasses splashes.

You never know what you're going to get out there and it's true that everybody is trying their best. But isn't it wonderful when you score a superstar? Waiters and waitresses who know the menu really well give us confident recommendations, informatively long pauses when you make a bad pick, and accurate three-dimensional air-hands portion-sized estimates.

It all adds up to a great night.

AWESOME!

30-second surprise neck and shoulder massages while cooking dinner at the end of a long day

My mom worked as an accountant in a mid-rise government building downtown. After long days squinting into tiny green-and-black computer screens, she'd lug the whole machine home in her **Chevrolet Cavalier** and step inside the front door sagging with exhaustion just before dinner.

Some days she'd lie face-down on the family room carpet and that was an invitation for my sister and I to begin our **clumsy tightrope walk** from her feet to her shoulders. Thirty pounds on the calves from Nina, forty pounds on the glutes from me, walking up and down our mom's back while Polkaroo popped over the fence on TV.

Sure, getting stepped on by tiny children may not have the full therapeutic benefits of a professional massage, but it more than makes up for it in love.

Touch is a deep human need and a **Surprise Massage** from a loved one in the middle of the day is a boost to the soul.

Before-bed heel squeezes from your mom, your boyfriend running his thumbs down your calves, and, oh yes, the deep joy of receiving a surprise 30-second massage while you're standing exhausted over a pot of steaming soup on the stove.

It all adds up to love.

AWESOME!

Gutsy city animals

....

Symbiosis ain't what it used to be.

When the neon-and-concrete jungles crash-landed on all the **ponds and tall grasses** it seems like one lanky species just stomped all the others away.

Since then, is it just me or does it sometimes get lonely living in the big city? I miss the days when wild horses woke you up in the morning, buffalo slept under your porch, and **upside-down possums** waved goodbye when you went to work.

Now everywhere you look it's just people, people, people.

I think that's why I was surprised one morning when I saw a flock of **tiny sparrows** picking away at crumbs and pebbles on the speedy on-ramp between two highways. Wedged between billboards, broken bottles, and glass towers, these little guys didn't have a care in the world. Eighteen-wheelers screaming by just inches away? No biggie! They were just gutsy city animals doing their thing.

It's refreshing when wild animals pop into city life because it reminds us this isn't our home—**we just live here**. Even though we've paved through the forest and plunked down massive towers, we really do need to pause and give props to the city animals gutsy enough to live with us.

Squirrels darting between delivery trucks, pigeons wandering across the street, and raccoons fist-fighting your dog for chicken bones all help remind us that our **paved paradise of**

put-up parking lots still allows for a rich world where we aren't the only ones doing the living.

Canada Goose, go ahead and lay your eggs behind the grocery store.

Seagull, squawk and swoop through the downtown core.

Armadillo, walk across the street even slower.

We're just glad you're here.

AWESOME!

COMMENTS:

Lee says:

I was walking to class one day and this squirrel cut me off high-tailing it with an entire extra-large slice of pizza in its mouth that was bigger than him/her!

Jdurley replies:

I have a pear tree, and one year an itinerant squirrel ate EVERY SINGLE PEAR, long before they were ripe. None of the other squirrels will eat them until they ripen more. But this one squirrel just got in there early and cleaned the tree right out. Thus proving the adage: the early squirrel gets the hard disgusting unripe pears.

Steve says:

I retired in Penang, Malaysia, which is an urban area with a population of over four million. I have seen five-foot-long monitor lizards, sun skinks, and even a cobra in my downtown condo parking lot!

Cheesy school photo day trends

Everybody's got a classic.

Buried in the basement, brass-framed on Grandma's staircase, I'm sure you can find a dusty 8 × 10 gem of a cheesy school photo featuring a cheesy school photo day trend:

- **That laser background.** Remember when the studio hired the local acid enthusiast to paint pink and blue laser backgrounds for a few years? There you were—bucktoothed and smiling in front of the light-bright abyss. Kids, this is what we thought the future looked like.
- **Old-school trendy hairstyle.** Whether you got the Nike Swoosh carved in the back of your buzz cut, crimped your bangs with a glittery headband, or had a wispy rat tail down to your shoulders, the point is that clearly you were the apex predator in the sixth grade food chain.
- **Forgot it was photo day photo.** This is the kid with the sideways bedhead, drool stains, or the one wearing a fraying Ultimate Warrior T-shirt with barbecue sauce on the collar. We feel bad for these kids on picture day, but they have the best photos thirty years later. Time is funny.
- **Posing with props.** It's the new grad with a gummy

smile holding a rolled-up diploma beside their head like a freshly caught trout. In case you couldn't tell by the black robe, square paper hat, or encyclopedia bookcase background, someone just got their last biology credit.

- **Braces smile.** You could always tell who had braces because their smile was an awkwardly forced, big-dimpled, tight-lipped beauty. Personally, I was always jealous of these kids since their physical deformity was easier to hide than foreheads full of pimples, donkey-gapped teeth, or a thick set of binocular glasses. Hypothetically, I mean.

- **Too dressed up for photo day photo.** This is the kid with perfectly braided hair, frilly pink dress, and knee-high socks. Or perhaps the crisp haircut, sweater vest, and bright red bow tie. Clearly their parents mixed up the picture day memo with their brunch invitation to Buckingham Palace.

It's always sweet pulling out old school photos and sharing connective smiles between your current and shadow selves.

Right between the side ponytails is a blurry and faded version of who you are right now in a tiny split-second moment way back in the middle of growing up.

AWESOME!

COMMENTS:

Laura says:

I had a few photos sporting that "We just had P.E. outside in gale-force winds and a slight drizzle right before this picture" look.

Heather says:

These are so true! And what about the one that was supposed to look like paint that had spilled? There was also one mom who dressed their kid in his Boy Scout uniform.

Jen says:

The thing I never liked during picture day was the random volunteer parent who would ALWAYS spit on their hand and try to adjust your hair to their liking.

Camiwa says:

Before my hair was chemically straightened my mom would straighten it with a hot comb. I wore my hair down for picture day, but the picture was taken AFTER recess. I must have gotten a little sweaty because my hair is ONE GIANT PUFF.

Finally finishing that scarf you started knitting a decade ago

··

And finally finishing thinking about it, too.
   AWESOME!

When the cake plops flawlessly out of the pan

....

It means three things.

First, you did it! You made a homemade cake. You wheeled your shopping cart past two-dollar mini-cupcakes with neon-green frosting, thirty chemicals listed under "Ingredients," and an expiration date in two years. Sure, the price was right, but you knew serving those would be like giving everybody a slice of tire.

Secondly, you mastered the oven. Do not overlook this point. Ovens routinely lie about temperature and have all kinds of **old man quirks** like tilted racks, missing burners, and anger management problems. I once pulled a Thanksgiving turkey out of the tiny old oven in my Boston apartment to find the entire bird cooked perfectly except for one completely raw leg. Twiddling temperatures, moving racks, and being careful not to open the door for **The Toothpick Test** too early means you are the Oven Maestro.

Lastly, when the cake comes out of the pan perfectly, it means you have no wasted crumbs. One of the few times gluttons and environmentalists really come together. Nobody is left sliding a fork down thin pan grooves to eke out a squiggly snake of partially uncooked batter. Sure, that's delicious, but the time spent coaxing an extra thousand molecules of uncooked cake is definitely much better spent with the **beaming birthday girl** in the backyard.

AWESOME!

Seeing your baby talk to themselves in the mirror like it's a completely different person

....

Hello baby, my old friend.

I've come to talk to you again.

Watching babies catch themselves in the mirror is the bit that never gets old. It starts with wide eyes and some finger pawing. Then they start trying to talk to the **Mirror Baby**. And then they slap the mirror and get a confused furrowed brow. They turn to you with a grunt that says, "Why is that other baby always interrupting me?"

I stare in my mirror every day looking for tiny imperfections. Spots, pimples, and wrinkles.

Watching my baby do it so blissfully carefree reminds me I should be looking for joy instead.

AWESOME!

—Jade Porter, Oklahoma City, Oklahoma

When you should have gotten a parking ticket but didn't

....

Well, well, well.

Look at you living life in the fire lane.

You came, **you parked**, you went over, and you know it.

Now you're scrambling out of the laundromat with a te-etery stack of folded towels, racing out of the barbershop with a freshly shorn neck, or running out of the pizza parlor with grease on your face and severe Pac-Man wrist.

When you get to the car you see the telltale signs: zeros flashing on the meter, tow trucks prowling the alleys, and meter maids swimming upstreet in the distance.

Your heart pounds as you race to your windshield and notice one big thing missing: **the parking ticket itself**.

There is no time for questions.

Jump into the driver's seat, shift your car into drive, and pound the gas so your tires squeal as you race straight out of town . . . race out of town . . . forever.

AWESOME!

Flossing

Skin-bleaching pastes in tiny heavy jars, spaceship-looking electric shavers that work in the shower, under-eye creams to remove wrinkles—we sure are surrounded by a lot of fancy and expensive personal hygiene technologies these days.

That's why flossing is so great.

It's just a piece of string.

AWESOME!

The couple minutes after the kids are buckled up but before you back out of the driveway

Enjoy a peaceful moment of
AWESOME!

The Moon

Everyone loves the sun.

Light, plants, tan lines, we get it, we get it.

But let's pause for a moment to say thanks to the other big guy in our sky. The moon is worth respecting for so many reasons:

1. **Lights up the night.** Next time you're lost on a camping trip, driving down a pitch-black country side road, or taking a midnight pee in the middle of nowhere, remember to look up and thank the moon for flashlighting all the twigs and branches so you don't tumble down the cliff.

2. **Get out of late free card.** I love seeing the moon still hanging around a clear blue morning sky. It's like that coffee shop employee in her winter jacket chilling behind the counter after her shift, pouring a few more drinks before heading home. "Yeah, yeah, I know the sun's here," she seems to say. "Just want to make sure everything's good before I leave." Plus, as everyone knows, it's impossible to be late for work when the moon's still out because it's not officially daytime yet. Be sure to check your Rules of Life pocketbook if you need clarification on this important matter.

3. **Toss the watch.** The moon's waxing and waning keeps our dates in check. Who needs Pope Gregory's Gregorian calendar from 500 years ago when the lunar calendar has kept things clear for 15,000 years? Relics dug up in France show we used eagle bones to track the lunar calendar 13,000 years ago and who knows how long before that. Our months are really just estimates of the lunar cycle, and *moon* and *month* come from the same root word.

4. **Let's get nuts.** To continue driving around Etymology Town, both *lunacy* and *loony* are derived from *Luna*, the Latin name for the Moon. Aristotle and Pliny the Elder thought full moons made people nuts because our brains are mostly water and therefore we get the same Earth-Moon tidal forces in our heads. Do you agree? Or think they were just two of the looniest among us? Feels like a good time to party, either way.

5. **Turn the tides.** Our moon is comparatively giant as far as moons go. There are 181 known moons in our solar system and our moon is the largest relative to its closest planet. The diameter of our moon is 25% of the Earth! Ganymede, the biggest moon in our solar system, is only 6% of Jupiter's diameter. Some researchers think our moon is an earlier chunk of Earth cracked off by an asteroid 4.5 billion years ago. Its oversized nature gives our planet such a strong gravitational yanking—sending tides up and down, waves in and out—that it creates mountainous peaks and deep ocean valleys all across the planet.

This makes Earth bumpy rather than smooth and is what allows land to exist. Said another way, without the moon, the entire surface of the Earth would be buried under water. That doesn't mean we wouldn't exist, necessarily. But we might be octopuses.

Sometimes our home planet can seem like a lonely base, **spinning in place**, floating through space. But when you stare out your bedroom window up into the distant forever reaches of infinite darkness, remember we've got a bright round friend riding with us everywhere we go.

The Moon's our lunchtime pal in the Universe Cafeteria and our seatmate at the back of the **Big Bang Bus**. So when it seems like the blackness is lonely, when it seems like we're far from home, just remember that the Moon's always with us . . . as we keep riding into the deep unknown.

AWESOME!

Dogs hanging their head out car windows

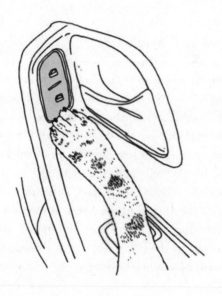

AWESOME!

Someone giving you a good idea on how to distract your kids for a solid hour so you can get some work done

....

"We got a good one," Abdalla said.

It was almost 11:00 p.m. and I was standing on the sidewalk fifteen feet down from him as he sat on a lawn chair on his front porch. Spring blooms lined the path between us and I felt a bit like I was suddenly alone in the **throne room** of a castle about to hear some wisdom from the wise old king. We had both had draining days at work so I had popped out of the house late to go for a walk and say hello in distanced times.

Sidewalks up and down the street were empty. TV screens kaleidoscoped like the **northern lights** through living room curtains. Flickering streetlights cast dim yellow shadows over our faces. It felt like the throne room was surrounded by giant **stained-glass windows** while a lightning storm raged down outside.

"Helena and I both had morning meetings at work and the boys are home right now so we asked them to organize the basement like a zoo," Abdalla said. "They made tickets, got dressed up, and had to classify and set up all their toys and stuffed animals by habitat. You know, reptile house, **boreal forest**, Asia pavilion, 'mythical creatures,' whatever."

I loved the idea and looked up at him for the big payoff.

He knew I wanted it.
He waited a moment.
And then he smiled.
And it finally came.
"It took them the whole morning!"
AWESOME!

Breakfast for dinner

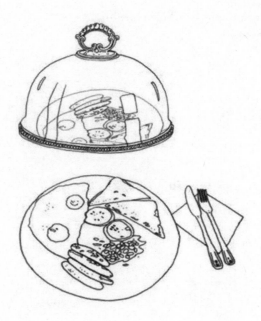

AWESOME!

When you're walking beside a fence or railing and you poke a stick in there so it just clangs over and over

....

It's like playing a harp with only one note.
  AWESOME!

Mastering the art of giving great rides

I look like a troll.

I am stout of construction with a shaggy beard, hunched posture, and long, troll-like arms.

There are some things I am not well suited to like running long distances, running short distances, and sharing armrests. But there are other things I am very well suited to, like lifting things really high, yelling loudly while popping my eyes out, and demanding people answer riddles so they can cross this bridge.

I am also well suited to throwing little children around safely.

It turns out I am the person every child wants to climb on and I take the responsibility seriously. I have a lot of practice with my kids and my nieces and nephews, but I'll warn you up front that the techniques below are dangerous and I recommend doing them in rooms filled with pillows. With that warning, let me share the top five rides for little ones:

1. **The Shoulder Ride.** This is a basic one that everyone needs in their tool-kit. You pick the kid up in a sitting position and sit them on your shoulders, with one leg on either side of your neck. You hold their legs so they stay on your shoulders. You can just carry them around this way or perform an equestrian-style

bouncing trot for extra spine-compressing jolts. Feel free to hurdle over a coffee table or park bench if you're feeling brave.

2. **The Head Ride.** A more advanced version of the Shoulder Ride. This one is the equivalent of getting to the top of the tower in your hometown and then paying the extra twenty bucks to go to the even higher level. "I bet the view is even better from there." Well, you're right. It is better. The child sits on top of your head, basket-of-water style, and you strongly hold their hips so they don't fall off. The best is playing a fun game of "Where's Amadeus? *Where's Amadeus?*" (Or whatever your kid is called.) Just watch for low doorframes and mud-smeared Keds to the teeth.

3. **Climb-Climb.** Climb-Climb involves holding your child's hands and assisting them to walk vertically up your body until they can either climb onto your head or do a shoulder-twisting backflip right back to the ground. Try not to do this one beside ponds or steep, jagged cliffs.

4. **Centrifugal Fun.** Grab your kid's hands and spin them round and round like a centrifuge. The name of the game is speed so extend your arms and lean back onto your heels for maximum g-forces. This one also doubles as a good warm-up for a follow-up game of Dizzy Tag.

5. **The Trampoline.** Lie on your back and let your kid take running knees-first jumps onto your stomach.

Your job is to try to catch them so they don't skid off your face into the coffee table. The real bonus is it doesn't take much energy and gets your child nicely warmed up for a long nap. The downside is you'll need a mouthguard and a jock.

It will take time and patience to slowly master these five rides. There's nothing to be embarrassed about if you plateau at Shoulder Ride or Climb-Climb for a while. Like any investment, the rewards are reaped over the long run.

Preferably before your kids get too fat.

AWESOME!

—*Darrell Lehouillier, Vancouver, British Columbia*

When that white noise you didn't know existed in the background suddenly stops

....

Shhhhhhhhhhhhhhhhhhhhhhhhhhhhhhhhhhhhhhhhhhhhhh
hhhhhhhhhhhhhhhhhhhhhhhhhhhhhhhhhhhhhhhhhhhhhhh
hhhhhhhhhhhhhhhhhhhhhhhhhhhhhhhhhhhhhhhhhhhhhhh
hhhhhhhhhhhhhhhhhhhhhhhhhhhhhhhhhhhhhhhhhhhhhhh
hhhhhhhhhhhhhhhhhhhhhhhhhhhhhhhhhhhhhhhhhhhhhhh
hhhhhhhhhhhhhhhhhhhhhhhhhhhhhhhhhhhhhhhhhhhhhhh
hhhhhhhhhhhhhhhhhhhhhhhhhhhhhhhhhhhhhhhhhhhhhhh
hhhhhhhhhhhhhhhhhhhhhhhhhhhhhhhhhhhhhhhhhhhhhhh
hhhhhhhhhhhhhhhhhhhhhhhhhhhhhhhhhhhhhhhhhhhhhhh
hhhhhhhhhhhhhhhhhhhhhhhhhhhhhhhhhhhhhhhhhhhhhhh
hhhhhhhhhhhhhhhhhhhhhhhhhhhhhhhhhhhhhhhhhhhhhhh
hhhhhhhhhhhhhhhhhhhhhhhhhhhhhhhhhhhhhhhhhhhhhhh
hhhhhhhhhhhhhhhhhhhhh

AWESOME!

Bailing on a sled

Yes, a rocky start and some poor weight distribution push your sled hard into the **slick and slippery snow**, which sprays sharp ice chunks into your eyes. Things get swervy when your buddy tumbles off the back and then you **completely lose control** while gaining speed just in time to see the creek bed coming up quickly in front of you.

You have no choice at this point. Even though it means smacking the ground hard, **spraining your ankle**, and tumbling down the hill, you just gotta do it.

Bail for the moment. Bail for the memories.

And bail for your life.

AWESOME!

Thick milkshakes and greasy fries at an old diner

With milkshakes made from rock-hard vanilla ice cream and fresh cold milk poured from a **big metal cup** into a heavy sundae-style glass and where they leave you the big metal cup after because it has more milkshake in it and then the outside gets all frosted before you pour the leftover **creamy lumpy** shake into your glass and where the fries are thick cut from real potatoes and served wet and glistening with hot oil and melting specks of salt on heavy and chipped white plates with **steel-wool scratches** and where ketchup comes from a half-empty bottle with smears crusting the top and where you need to pound the sides with your wrist ten times to get it to suddenly gush out and where you're swiveling on **burgundy vinyl stools** while leaning on a smooth worn counter with little stars and diamonds on it and where you feel like you're eating with ghosts of your past and dreams of the future and the whole scene just feels incredibly
AWESOME!

Starting the lawn mower on the first pull

Time for a trim.

Step into those grass-stained boots, **toss on a faded ball cap**, and scrape open the doors of your wobbly tin shed. Push past the cracked kiddie pool and cobweb-covered patio chairs until you find the rusty mower with the grass-covered wheels and pull it right on out.

Now, if you're like me, then before pulling the cord you sort of get it in your mind that you're in for three or four **full-body yanks** before the machine starts purring. I don't know about you, but since I'm a small **noodle of a man** I find pulling that cord about as draining as bench-pressing a full keg of beer, building a house out of boulders, or dragging one of those giant rubber tires up a steep hill with a rope.

I generally put my whole body into it and just get some slow sputtering. It's like the machine is taunting me. "Oh, you're gonna need to pull harder than that," it says, before adding, "and I've successfully weakened you before you do it."

But hey, that's what makes it great when us noodles pull those cords and they start up on the first pull. Now when the motor starts whirring and the gas fumes start floating, we suddenly get to feel like the **World's Strongest Humans**.

Pass the black spandex shorts, **tattoo skulls on our necks**, and toss us some barbells, baby.

We're going in.

AWESOME!

Taking a nap after eating pancakes

We have a strange relationship with breakfast.

We scramble eggs. We cook oatmeal. We smear peanut butter onto seedy bread. And yet, somehow, at the same time, we also feel like this is the meal to make a couple **giant towers of doughy cakes** before dousing them in syrup.

Don't get me wrong! I'm not complaining. Pancakes for breakfast is something I can get behind. Just one request.

Before we do the dishes and get on with the rest of our Saturday, can we just pause for like three hours to take a giant nap on the couch?

AWESOME!

Making the last-second call to grab an umbrella on your way out the door this morning

And then being totally vindicated when it starts raining on your way home.

AWESOME!

Actually finishing a bar of soap

Work that hard rectangle into a soft-cornered bar.

Work that soft-cornered bar into a smooth oval.

Work that smooth oval into a thin bar with deep creases.

Work that thin bar with deep creases into a jagged and splintery soap icicle.

And now it's time for the big decision:

Option 1: Throw it out. Maybe you look at the jagged and splintery soap icicle as the chicken bone of the soap. This is as low as you can go. It was a good run. There's no shame in giving it a noble burial in the garbage can full of Q-tips and Kleenexes under the sink.

Option 2: Soap surgery. Here's where you attempt to extend the soap's life span by grafting it onto the back of a new bar. Get everything wet, squeeze it all together, and hope for a couple weeks of patience, care, and empathetic houseguests. Or the soap might die on the table. One false move and it's down the drain. Now the life-support machine flatlines and you pound your fist on the sink and angrily toss your scrubs in the trash. It's not fair! It's just not fair!

Option 3: Going all the way. This is the ultimate move where you manage to work the jagged soap icicle until it's completely gone. Note this may require weeks of scrubbing your hands with dime-sized shards of soap between your fingers for five minutes and getting essentially no lather. Remember your soap is giving it all it can here. It has almost nothing left. Just smile and admire its beauty and will.

AWESOME!

COMMENTS:

....

Rhys says:

My auntie puts them all in an old stocking and ties the stocking to the tap in her laundry. Feels just like another cake of soap but it's just full of the leftover bits.

> *Mia replies:*
>
> Yes, I take all the little pieces of soap and put them in a pretty basket in my linen closet. Makes the towels and sheets smell nice and I haven't wasted anything!

Thomas says:

What about actually finishing a stick of Chapstick? I have never done it but I imagine it's pretty awesome!

> *Jdurley replies:*
>
> Eventually you get to the stage where you can't wind it up any higher and you have to start digging little nuggets out with your fingernails.

Emily replies:

The only way I ever come close to finishing one is if I have one, lose it for a few months, find it, lose it again, find it again, etc.

Jose says:

Soap Surgery is not hard if you do it right. Make sure there's a bit of water left in the soap dish to soak the leftover sliver, then when it's soft, plop the fresh one on top. Flip over, let dry, and you have a solid new bar with an oddly shaped bump on it.

Freddo says:

My wife and I have very different ideas of when it's time to replace the soap with a new bar. We usually get to a point where I go with a new bar of soap, and she continues to use the thin bar (and eventually the scraps) for weeks. By that time, I've whittled the full bar down to a point where I won't use it anymore, and she inevitably starts using the resulting scraps again. Poor wife—she never ends up using a full bar of soap.

When it's snowing and it sticks to the grass but not the pavement
—Michelle Hedstrom

When your puppy is victorious in killing the squeaky part of her toy
—Marlene Meyer

Your teen son saying "I love you" when hanging up the phone even when he's with his friends
—Cassie Glasgow

When you have something in the microwave and toaster at the same time and they finish and beep in unison
—Hillary Anne

Cooking for a loved one who's just been released after 27 years of incarceration
—Kathryn Parr

Interviewing with a panel of female leaders within a company for a new job and then having my property manager and her assistant come by to fix the water heater in my apartment for a full day of female empowerment
—Chelsea Perry

Thinking your passport expires soon but it's good for five more years
—Tanya Linau

When you pull into the parking lot listening to a great song and when you walk into the store they have their radio tuned to the same station
—Dara Smida

Getting all the chocolates you want from the box of assorted chocolates

My first girlfriend may have been an alien.

She looked normal, she dressed normal, she seemed normal, but she liked those oozing cherry-syrup-in-the-middle chocolates from the chocolate box. The ones wrapped in gold foil and stuffed with that bizarre, mutant **sugar-cherry** that looked like it was steeped in the garbage cans outside the nuclear power plant.

Those were her favorite!

Clearly, whenever we were splitting a box of assorted chocolates, I always scored my first pick: the dream combo of strawberries and cream. I loved those **goopy pink innards** oozing out and had no shame drilling into the second layer to mine all the artificially flavored strawberry in the box. (You know you're sharing with a pro when one specific chocolate is missing on both levels.)

What about you?

Do you like the extra chewy fudgy ones that get stuck in your molars all day like fillings? Do you prefer those flaky imitation coconut squares? Do you hunt ruthlessly for the one chocolate truffle, get your vitamin C fix with orange cream, or just pop the lid off and swipe the boring rectangle of milk chocolate sitting in the middle?

Whatever your pleasures, whatever your tastes, we both know it's a beautiful moment when you score all the chocolate you want from the box you're sharing with somebody.

Nothing is worse than when your kid brother loses the legend page and you're forced to play **Russian Choclette** with your picks.

It means you might end up with the cherry.

Nabbing your favorite chocolate from the box?

AWESOME!

Spinning in an office chair for no reason

AWESOME!

When one of your paintings or tests makes it onto the fridge

When you get the itch to go for it, you can go all the way to the top. No one will tell you to stop! Study and study, try and try, dream to go far, wish to go high. Go for it, go for it, believe it can be, enjoy the feeling of no limits on what you can achieve. And on the way there make sure to enjoy small victories best, like when your dad puts a magnet on your A+ math test. Yes, every time mom puts something on the fridge in the kitchen, it keeps those dreams dreaming and keeps those wishes wishing.

AWESOME!

The silence after the bone-shaking noise stops

Everywhere I ever try to find a quiet place to write, apparently, there's a construction crew with some **urgent jackhammering** or buzz-sawing or metal-bashing to do, right outside my window. In Brooklyn, it was new condo developments; in the Yorkshire countryside, where I live now, it's people converting **historic barns** into living spaces. But it comes with an unexpected flip side: that special, somehow deeper and richer silence that descends once the noise stops and the crews go home.

You can feel it, likewise, when the truck idling on the street outside finally drives away. Or when you're visiting **Edinburgh, Scotland**, and one of the buskers who plays bagpipes on a street corner decides to take a tea break. (Sorry, Scottish buskers, but it's true. Bagpipes were designed for *warfare*, and I'm a man of peace.)

In each of those moments, a background anxiety that I wasn't quite conscious of feeling gives way to glorious relief. And as a result, I'm plunged more fully into the moment than I would have been if things had simply been silent all along.

I don't think we pay enough attention to relief as an emotion in general. Our **peppy, positive-thinking culture** is predisposed to seeing joy as something you need to create, or add to life. But relief is a reminder that, often enough, the joy is already there.

It's just that sometimes you—and those construction crews—need to get out of its way.

Of course, the expert level would be to find joy in the sounds of the jackhammering, too. I'm working on that. For now, I'll settle for the glorious moment that it stops.

AWESOME!

—*Oliver Burkeman, North York Moors, England*

When you're not the new guy anymore

That first day was scary.

When you opened the door, everything was a giant swirling abyss of new teachers, new faces, new rules, new places. You tiptoed in, smiling and shaking hands, learning passwords and policies, and staring around the busy cafeteria holding your **red plastic tray** just hoping to make eye contact with someone.

It wasn't your fault, but you were last to join the team, you were last getting in the game, you were the last one who got hired, and no one knew your name.

So you just put your head down and gave it a shot. **You tried and tried and tried.** You weren't sure if you belonged here, so maybe you worked harder than the next guy. You organized a neighborhood yard sale, **helped the bullpen in the clutch**, bailed us all out of a big meeting, or threw a backyard party . . . with a special touch.

(Special touches may or may not include: big bowls of fizzy punch filled with sliced oranges, skewers of meat pulled out of a smoky tandoor, or a tissue-paper-covered donkey piñata.)

Soon you noticed you were starting to fit in and there were beers after the ball game, **lab partners in chemistry class**, and new friends in the cafeteria. Somebody asked you for help one day, a nickname slowly evolved, and a joke you told kept everyone laughing for weeks.

One day someone even newer than you started up and when

you saw them staring around the busy cafeteria holding their red plastic tray it suddenly hit you that you're not the new guy anymore.

You've come a long way and now you're part of this place.

Now wave them over, pull out a chair, and invite them into the

AWESOME!

Food gawking

....

Check out that sexy plastic orange tray.

Welcome to the crowded food court, workplace lunchroom, or high school cafeteria. Thin napkins and ketchup smears cover tables as wailing babies and **french fry fumes** fill the air. It's time for lunch so your stomach's grumbling and all you can think about is how hungry you are.

That's when it happens.

A man walks by and all you see are his steamed buns. A woman strolls past and all you notice are her enchiladas. Then someone runs over your foot with their wheelchair but you're too hypnotized by their **spring rolls** to feel any pain.

Eyes pop and drool drips as you stand spinning in a neon daze. This is modern day hunting and you're tray ogling with the finest. You know you're **food gawking** when one of these classic moments happens:

1. **The Shoulder Tap.** You're dining out with friends and you spot a couple eating something good by the window. You stare down at your menu and discover that it's . . . just text! No steaming stir-fries or scrambled slams staring up at you. Now you eyeball their meals and casually stroll by on your way to the bathroom to see what's cooking. If you're like me, you try and fail to find their meal on the menu. "They've got

something covered in cheese and tomato sauce over there . . . but I don't see anything like that." Now you give a guilty smile and shoulder-tap the waiter for help. Or for Bonus Rudeness Points you can yell across the room to ask. Maybe clink your fork on your saucer a few times to get their attention.

2. **The Bad Trade.** After reuniting with your pals at the plastic food court table under the beach-themed umbrella you notice three of you got cold sandwiches full of green uncored tomatoes and limp lettuce pathetically hanging out the sides and the other person came back with a steaming plate of hot lasagna and fresh garlic bread. You slip into lasagna hypnosis and go for a massively unbalanced trade. "Six inches of my sub for just one bite. And you can have my bag of chips, too!" Did they say yes? Good. Now try peeling off as much cheese as you can.

3. **The Lazy Man's Regret.** There's always one person willing to wait ten minutes at the made-to-order pasta station in the cafeteria or the omelet station at the hotel buffet. Sure, you think she's a fool at first, but after she sits down you can't help but look over at her plate and curse your impatience. "I, too, could have had an egg white omelet with Swiss cheese and freshly foraged mushrooms." Tears spill as you think about the rubbery pancakes and wet, gritty, reconstituted scrambled eggs you just filled your stomach with.

4. **The Unobtainable Leftovers.** A stack of microwaves in the office cafeteria is a leftovers fashion show. You stuff your tasteless freezer-burned chili in while drooling over the bright green pea and chewy-cheesy matar paneers and salty beef-and-oniony phos popping out of the other machines. These meals are not accessible to you. There's no line to wait in. There's no money to pay. So you're stuck staring like a food-gawking fool.

When we're hungry, stomachs rule and all meetings, notifications, and texts fade to the background. Now it's time to food gawk and fill your stomach by spotting ice cream sources, sniffing steaming coffees, and walking back till you find those greasy snacks.

AWESOME!

That bend in the pipe under the sink

Do your business outside.

This was an unspoken law our species followed as we built our earliest clay huts half a million years ago. When nature called in the middle of the night you slipped outside and stepped past mastodon bones till you found a tree.

Rules changed after public water supplies and **pressurized well systems** came around a few hundred years ago and we started outfitting rich people's pads with indoor plumbing. Sounds good? Well, sure, except for one big problem: **the smell**. Turns out that sticking pipes in your house and draining them straight into sewers underground sort of makes your castle smell like Fart Perfume.

Who knew?

Great Scot Alexander Cummings, that's who. He put his finger on his chin and stared up to the ceiling back in 1775 before saying, "Let's put a bend in the pipes. That'll trap water in there, which will block smells from filling our homes." His wonderful idea came with the side benefit that if you ever drop a **wedding ring** or a diamond necklace down the drain, there's a good chance it'll get caught in that bend in the pipe and your family jewels won't get washed out to sea.

So take a whiff today and if your home smells okay, just stop to say thanks to **Big Al** from a few hundred years ago.

AWESOME!

Finding your name on some tacky souvenir in the gift shop

....

Bob, Betty, Brian, you don't know the shame.

Bilal, Bryanna, Bao-Tian, you know the pain of turning that **squeaky metal frame** full of plastic doorplates and failing to find your name.

My friend Agostino tells a great story about how one day he found his dad's name on a toothbrush in Italy. He was on vacation and was stunned to find that somebody stamped "Guido" on a toothbrush.

To this day his dad says it's his favorite present of all time. AWESOME!

Seeing your teacher in the grocery store and suddenly realizing they are a real person

....

When I was a kid, I couldn't imagine any primary school teacher outside of the classroom. It's like they were caged animals in **sweater vests** who had no life outside of teaching fractions, rhyming couplets, or a three-week unit on owls.

I knew we occasionally saw them drive away but I assumed they were going to **buy chalk** before returning to class, getting into a sleeping bag in the supplies closet, and dozing off in front of the flap-flap-flap of the film projector.

Gradually, over the years, I discovered little things that would create suspicions about their alien life form.

"Who's Joan? What do you mean Miss McKay is Joan? Then who's Miss McKay?"

They slowly hinted at the life beyond our yellow cinderblock walls. They'd mention a favorite musician (anything other than Nana Mouskouri seemed out of character), talk about a book they had read (why were they reading anything other than Roald Dahl?), or post a new photo of a wife or husband beside their desk. Sure, there were hints, but after collusion on everything from Santa Claus to "math is really important," I didn't trust them. They could have been grown in a factory for all I knew.

And then it happened.

The thing that rocked my world more than anything else.

I saw a teacher at a grocery store.

It blew my mind, made me question everything, and led me to believe I was living in a multiverse.

How was this possible?

She had left her plastic wobbly chair, **green-carpeted**, paint-splotched easel habitat and was right here in civilization.

Buying a melon.

That's when it all became clear to me.

Teaching me wasn't all she did. She was a real person. With real friends, needs, and dreams. She had real challenges. She suffered real pain. **She shed real tears.** Maybe she said things she regretted to her sister, maybe she missed her mother, maybe she daydreamed about her life bouncing in a dozen different directions from here.

But, for now, here she was: human, beautiful, offering a passionate and loving part of herself to me and my classmates . . . every single day.

AWESOME!

—*Ron Tite, Oshawa, Ontario*

Hands-Free Everything public bathrooms

....

Nobody wants to touch rusty urinal flushes, crusty soap pumps, and germ-covered bathroom door handles. Which is why the rare Hands-Free Everything public bathroom is the true holy grail of sanitation. To pull it off we're going to need all these family favorites:

1. **Zig-zagging bathroom entrances.** Top marks are awarded for bathrooms that do not even have a door. Awkward lineup moves and crumpled paper towel piles are all nonexistent because the designer threw in a simple Hallway 180 that keeps the bathrooms private and the entrances entirely hands-free.
2. **Self-flushing toilets.** Anyone who has ever waited in a bathroom lineup of sweaty guys between periods at the hockey game will agree that self-flushing toilets are a critical advancement for humanity. Bonus points for the jet-engine-loud ones that send toddlers screaming. Or the extremely rare Japanese self-cleaning seat.
3. **Automatic faucets.** Bottom rung are the ones shooting six painful needle-thin streams of freezing water with one stream always shooting sideways. Middle

rung are elementary-school-style half-circle sinks with a black rubber foot pedal that turns on the faucets. Top rung are the simple black sensors that always work and gush out floods of warm water.

4. **Automatic soap dispensers.** If all the automatic bathroom machines are sitting down for family dinner, the soap dispenser is definitely the crazy uncle. He's completely unpredictable, always shoots his mouth off, and frankly cannot be trusted. Pink sink smears and foam explosions on the mirror show his wild side. But he's part of the family. We need him, we respect him, we love him for who he is.

5. **Hand-sensor paper towels.** Hand dryers should be banished from the world. Yes, I said it. I'm sorry, environmentalists, but you know it's true. We need a quick wipe here—not thirty seconds of frantically rubbing our hands under wheezing lukewarm air. And don't make us swipe past the red sensor for three inches of paper towel and then give us a forced flashing twenty-second pause. We want the classy service-oriented dispensers that have a long sheet waiting for us, and then, after we swipe, out comes a fresh sheet ready for the next guy.

Hands-Free Everything public bathrooms, people.
Cleanliness, freedom, and the dawn of a new day.
What a time to be alive.
AWESOME!

Being the guy on the roadside construction crew who gets to hold the Stop sign

When I drive by roadside construction workers, I just can't believe what's happening.

Everyone's face is coated in a layer of hot soot, sewer grease, and sweat. One guy is up to his neck in **The Road**, another is jackhammering his spinal column to dust, and then there's this third guy driving the **big roller**—spreading steaming asphalt around like butter. Around these folks are those guys **smashing pickaxes** into the ground and others steering massive bulldozers down narrow gravel shoulders beside steep sewer ditches.

And, of course, the whole gang is losing brain cells by the minute from what smells like a gas station full of jammed laser printers.

If you're on a roadside construction crew, I think you're pretty lucky if they hand you the job of **being the guy who gets to hold the Stop sign**. Sometimes you tell cars to stop. Sometimes you tell cars to go. Do you think you can handle it?

Maybe you're the grizzled veteran who earned every hour of the Stop sign job with every slipped disc over the years or maybe you're the baby-faced newbie who nobody trusts within a quarter mile of the job site.

Just enjoy the moment of relief.

AWESOME!

Peak magnolia

....

I remember like it was yesterday.

I was pushing my young son on the **baby swings** at the park every day as the weather warmed and looking at the old magnolia tree across the street, which was starting to bloom. Jigsaw branches hung a wide canopy over the neighbor's wet and thawing lawn. Long and furry **green pods** sprouted and thickened and some were starting to reveal the pink and white grapefruit-sized blossoms growing inside.

Then the snowstorm hit.

"What will happen to the tree?" my older son asked that night after the baby had gone to sleep. Big bowls of stew steamed in front of us as the freak blizzard raged out the window. "I don't know, son," I said quietly, while staring into the crackling fire. Neither of us said another word that night.

The next morning we went to see the tree.

We could tell before we got there.

Everything was coated in snow and ice.

Poor thing didn't stand a chance.

As the weather warmed again the tree gave many strong efforts to bloom. But the flowers that blossomed were covered in **brown splotches** and most gave up and snapped off before blooming, anyway. The tree looked bare and the lawn ended up covered in unopened buds lying on a thin crust of snow with blades of grass shooting through.

The next spring I pushed my son on the **big-kid swing** and we watched nervously as the old magnolia started blooming. Sure enough, furry green pods sprung out and after weeks of anticipation . . . the blossoms slowly punctured the **bare brown branches** with pink dots and then a gorgeous white-and-pink flooding of flowers.

It's soul-filling to remember how rare and fragile and beautiful and precious it is seeing an old magnolia tree in absolute peak bloom.

Apple trees, **peony bushes**, cherry trees, whatever you enjoy near you—let's remember to stare in wonder as these giant planted peacocks spread their glorious wings.

AWESOME!

Sleep lines

Sleep lines are any line left on your skin after waking up.

Arm dents from **pillow case zippers** and cheek creases from crumpled sheets pair well with sideways bedhead and distant slow-blinking gazes out the window with your adorable rosy-red cheeks.

Sleep lines tell the world you just had a great nap.

For bonus points add drool stains.

AWESOME!

Lineup Friends

....

Have you ever waited in a really, really long line? I'm not talking ten minutes getting to the bathroom at halftime, fifteen minutes for popcorn on opening night, or even twenty minutes sliding through security in socks.

No, I'm talking about lineups more than half an hour, sometimes more than an hour, sometimes more than two. I'm talking about forever-long lines at **brand new amusement park rides**, outside the DMV on Monday mornings, or down the empty road alongside that **sketchy old warehouse** before doors open to the concert.

If you're stuck in a really long line you probably do what I do and talk with people you know or send three hundred texts. But at some point you get bored. Batteries die, **conversations dry**, and you're twiddling your thumbs. And that's when the four-step process to making Lineup Friends comes in handy:

> **Step 1: We can have lots of fun** . . . by complaining about the line together! Somebody moans about the wait and a stranger chimes in. "Seriously, are we even moving?" "Yeah, like did they not plan for this?" Suddenly we're in this together! How dare they make *us* wait? We shake our fists against the invisible amusement park titans. You now have a Lineup Posse.

Step 2: There's so much we can do. Lineup Acquaintances typically have lots in common. Are you waiting outside a punk show? Talk about your fresh piercings. Are you in line at the art gallery for the new exhibit? Discuss how expensive floor mats are for your Audis.

Step 3: It's just you and me. Step 3 involves talking with your new friend all the way to the front of the line. Does your new friendship seem to have the ability to jump topics a few times? Is there nicely shared airspace? Do we value similar things? Listening deepens connection. Vulnerability makes an appearance here.

Step 4: I can give you more. Swapping contact details seals the friendship. Too risky asking your new Lineup Friend for their number? Ask for an email to send them that photo you just took or to get that movie recommendation you were just talking about. This invites your friendship into the post-line dimension to see if the organic connection may continue to grow.

We live in the echo chambers of our own making, so it's great breaking out of the **smeary dreary** into fresh territory. Lineup Friends make time pass, keep the jokes coming, and brighten our days with new connections.

Line up, friends!

You won't regret it.

AWESOME!

Old-school sugar cereals

....

Let's go back.

Sandy pink streaks coat the sky as the sun peeks over your backyard fence and rays reflect off the orange and brown linoleum of the kitchen floor. Oven burners wobble and pop, the fridge murmurs and hums, and you enjoy a few moments alone with a box of sugar cereal.

Let's count down ten of the greatest cereals of all time:

10. **Corn Pops.** The delayed-time-release technology allowed sticky yellow chunks to remain in your molars until you needed energy for later in the day. Very handy because, sometimes in the middle of math class, you just gotta have your pops.

9. **Trix.** I always felt bad for the rabbit. Didn't it seem to you like all the toddlers were jerks? "Silly rabbit," they laughed, with their cold, beady eyes, right in his face. "Trix are for kids." Come on, he just wants a bowl of cereal. These are probably the same punks who stole Lucky's Charms.

8. **Sugar Crisp.** Did anyone else think Sugar Bear was a distant cousin of Chester Cheetah? Think about it—the sunglasses, the long strides, the sneakers? Chilled-out dudes who ditched jungle living for Hollywood's big bucks? Roommates at least.

7. **Cocoa Pebbles, Cocoa Puffs, or Count Chocula.** Did you ever get away with having a bowl of chocolate for breakfast? Good one to pour extra milk in so you end with a chocolate milk chaser.

6. **Grape-Nuts.** Okay, this isn't a sugar cereal, but didn't you always have a stale box kicking around from when Grandma visited? Nobody knew what a Grape-Nut was, either. We'd just quietly pass the box around on those dark mornings when the sugar ran dry and we were forced to suddenly consider our colorectal health. Shredded Wheat or All-Bran sometimes made cameos, too. Grape-Nuts helped us dream about tomorrow's Froot Loops, Frosted Flakes, and Cinnamon Toast Crunch. They're on the list because they made the next bowl sweeter.

5. **Honeycomb.** Remember the TV commercial where the angry biker in a Viking helmet storms the kids' forest hideout and starts a group sing-a-long with a dancing robot? Combine that with a few episodes of *The Smurfs* and you've got a very trippy Saturday morning. "Honeycomb's big—yeah, yeah, yeah!— it's not small—*no, no, no!*"

4. **Lucky Charms.** First off, the gang at General Mills redefined marshmallow to mean rock-hard bits of dyed, packed sugar. And then seemed to invent new shapes all the time. Pink hearts, yellow moons, shooting stars all turned the milk magically delicious.

3. **Cap'n Crunch.** My friend Chad once told me he didn't learn the right way to spell "captain" until he was a

teenager. Also, did you know Cap'n Crunch was one of the few cereals to feature an arch-nemesis in their ads? Yes, you may recall the Soggies coming around and attempting to prematurely dampen your cereal. To stop them you had to scarf down your bowl in under sixty seconds and leave the roof of your mouth shredded for the rest of the day.

2. **Cookie Crisp.** This was just a big box full of tiny cookies. If your mom fell for this, do you think she'd let us bum some cigarettes and borrow her car?

1. **Honey Nut Cheerios.** Perhaps the most delicious of all the sugary milks. Most kids had a long run with this faithful classic. Smooth corners made for easy chomping and you could toss a handful in a baggie for a takeout snack. Plus the false suggestion of "nuts" made them sound a bit healthier, too.

Depending on how you grew up, eating some sugar cereal might have occurred during some quiet time before the school day began. While parents rushed around and the radio blared traffic reports, you read the back of the box and then fished around for the sticker at the bottom before your sister got it.

Sure, old-school sugar cereals weren't healthy, but those vitamin-fortified sugar punches made for mighty fun childhoods.

AWESOME!

COMMENTS:

....

Nick says:

When I was a child, I would sneak the brand new box of Lucky Charms from the pantry and eat every single marshmallow. The next day, upon finding no marshmallows in the box, my mother would just look at me and slowly shake her head.

> *Mike replies:*
>
> You're the opposite of the kids who only got sugar cereal in multipack single serve boxes when they went camping. Last kid out of the tent? Poor bastard got Bran Flakes.

Sal says:

When we went to the cottage (only once a summer as it was a nine-hour drive) my brothers and I each got to pick a box of "crap cereal," as my dad called them. So three of us negotiated who would pick what in order to get best of the best. No point in picking two chocolate flavors, as it's going to be another year till we tear open the roofs of our mouths again.

"My 10-year-old started reading *The Book of Awesome* and has started her own list, which includes 'Convincing your parents to order out for dinner,' 'Being able to have a soda that you usually can't have,' and 'Indoor plumbing' (that one came after our visit to Yellowstone). Her list is already about 50 items long! She is newly motivated to read!"

—*Laura from Virginia*

Sleeping in on weekend mornings

AWESOME!

Holding a baby in one arm while successfully making an entire breakfast with the other

··

Crying babies call.

Do you leave **Soggy Wetcheeks** screaming in the high chair for five minutes while you spin around frying eggs? No, you don't, because where's the challenge in that? It's time to pick up the baby, yank open the fridge, and get breakfast going.

Start by tilting all your weight onto one wobbly leg while grabbing some eggs. Are your glutes burning? We're just getting started here. Now you need to keep the eggs out of baby's **swinging wingspan** before setting them on the counter and then keep an eye on them in case of rolling while also curling your toes to pull open the heavy bottom drawer under the stove. Squeeze your obliques, move baby onto your other hip, tilt onto your other leg, and grab the frying pan with a sharp side bend.

Keep your core tight!

Are your baby's eyes wide in excitement? Or is that horror? No time to assess! Turn on the stove before performing a dramatic deep-seated squat to **jump-twist** for the butter dish from the other counter. Are your hamstrings screaming? Can't quit now. Hurry up and use one hand to slice a smear of butter off and scrape it on the edge of the frying pan while using the other to bounce the baby. Now rip the tag off the bread and drop a couple of slices into the toaster before the butter in the frying pan starts sizzling.

Are you done? No, it's time for the quad lutz—the most difficult move of your morning! Everybody knows what's coming and there is an audible gasp from the crowd as you lean back into a **wobbly one-legged dead lift**, grab an egg, and then majestically crack it on the side of the pan, spread the broken shells out (one-handed), and gently let the eggs drop into the pan without breaking the yolk.

Your child is being raised by an Olympian.

AWESOME!

Anything served to you sizzling or on fire at a restaurant

....

It started with murgh mirch tikka.

In my mid-20s I was living with my parents in the suburbs and began carpooling downtown most weekends with my friend Stephen. He drove a bright teal Pontiac Sunfire and we'd sing along to the appropriately colored *Blue Album* by Weezer and scream "Feel the teeeeeeeal!" whenever we passed someone on the highway. I have so many fond memories of weekend jams featuring birthday dinners at packed restaurants and many late nights full of sweaty dancing and 3:00 a.m. street meat.

A few of our friends loved Indian food, so every few months we'd end up at a **samosa-filled joint** filled with pillowy soft naans and steaming curries, the scents soaking deeply into our hair and clothes. Whenever we ate there Stephen would always order **murgh mirch tikka**, which was just three massive hunks of blackened sizzling chicken coated in a spicy deep green marinade. He would talk about it for weeks in advance and always order another one to go before we left, stashing it in the trunk of the Sunfire for brunch the next morning. Sure, it was delicious, but I can't explain his **torrid love affair** except to say that it sure is great when anything is served to you sizzling or on fire at a restaurant.

Let's count down some other classics:

1. **Chicken fajitas.** I absolutely love getting that clay-colored plastic dish full of tortillas with a burning black plate covered in sizzling chicken, peppers, and onions. Stephen always ordered a burrito and insisted fajitas were just a way for the kitchen to outsource labor. "I came here to eat," he'd say, "not spend half my time building dinner." Sure, the man had a point, but Stephen's fat burrito wasn't saying much while I enjoyed my sizzles.

2. **Saganaki.** Have you had this at a Greek restaurant? A hot pan of extremely salty cheese lit on fire just before it's served to you? Perfect for anyone hoping to destroy their appetite by opening their meal with a dense oily brick to the gut. Opa!

3. **Rice Krispies at a motel buffet.** Okay, maybe we've hit rock bottom by counting cereal, but sometimes Rice Krispies beat everything else at the cheap continental buffet. Keep your watered-down orange drink and shiny, rock-hard muffin in the cellophane bag. We'll be snap, crackle, popping in the corner.

4. **Korean grilling.** The thin strips of beef at a Korean grill are served raw, but they get sizzling when you toss them in that grill built into the middle of your table. It's very simple: toss them in, eat them up, go home happy.

5. **Dessert on fire.** Now, I have never actually had this, but I've heard tales of banana flambés and rum-soaked cakes lit on fire and brought to the table. I assume it's best enjoyed after a dinner of saganaki

and chicken fajitas with a flaming shot of sambuca on the side.

Next time you're served anything sizzling or on fire at a restaurant, take a moment to pause and look around the room. Conversation stops and eyebrows rise as everybody's eyes flick orange and red in a beautiful ten seconds of
AWESOME!

Having a great story to go with that horrible bruise

··

I once played badminton with my friend Jon.

Turns out he was a member of the local racket (*hey-ohhhh!*) and was in the business of casually inviting friends to join him for a night as his **Doubles Partner**.

Now badminton, like most sports, was completely foreign to me so I had a pile of excuses ready when he asked me to play, including: "I don't have a racquet," "I don't have a ball," "I don't know how to play," and finally my loyal and trusty fail-safe, "No."

Jon would have none of it.

"Come on, I'll pick you up and drop you off. I have an extra racquet and I'll bring you a bottle of water. Plus, the guys there are really easygoing and casual. You'll have a great time. It'll be fun."

There was a bit of a standoff as we sized each other up, squinted a bit, and jutted our chins out, but eventually I sucked it up, threw on some sweatpants, and went along for the ride.

Turns out Jon was a liar.

I entered the dimly lit high school gym to the sight of high-flying **Asian superstars** spiking the birdie in all directions. Zipping and zooming across the court, they leapt two, three, four feet off the ground, whacking the bird in high-stakes, high-drama, back-and-forth exchanges.

"Oh, it's not as tough as it looks," Jon said to my suddenly pale face. "And don't worry—no one cares how good you are. They just want to get some exercise."

I stared at Jon with a worried glance, but eventually unpeeled my racquet, yanked up my tube socks, and stepped shivering onto the court, where I proceeded to immediately get beaned in the eye by a well-smacked birdie. Yes, I'm telling you straight up: **I got shuttlecocked bad**.

It happened fast. I dropped my racquet, stunned, cupping my eye with both hands while sucking air in loudly like a vacuum. Throbbing, swelling, bruising fast, I was experiencing the birth of my first-ever **black eye**.

Thick, dark, purple, yellow, and navy blue, I sported the fat shiner for the next couple weeks at work. And while I'm well aware big bruises can be signs of serious issues, and we should always take care to lovingly check in with people who may have experienced something horrible, I have to tell you that in my situation . . . the black eye felt great. It wasn't terribly sore. My eye was fine. And the bruise was liberating and identity-expanding. I felt like I had busted free from my wimpy shackles!

For a brief moment, I wasn't a **thin, fragile little bird** but a street tough with an attitude problem. Okay, the street was more of a rat maze of cubicle hallways and the tough guy was actually, you know, Neil from Human Resources, but I did enjoy trying on a new self.

To cope with the exhaustion of the infinite we flatten and two-dimensionalize each other, which helps us to "stay in our lane" so algorithms can better anticipate and corral our behavior into predictable clicks. **It's harder to hear our own voice in the**

noise. Walking around with a black eye to me back then was like showing up to Thanksgiving dinner with a shaved head, dating someone outside your parents' comfort zone, or finally flying off to that country you've been dreaming about since you were a kid.

Letting perceptions and ideas of who we are briefly fall away helps us see what's behind the curtain in our minds and experience the world from new perspectives.

AWESOME!

Eating a taco without anything falling out

....

I always break my taco's back.

Yes, before I bite my hard-shell taco, a loud splintery crack fills the air and I notice I've just given my taco a **career-ending spinal injury** by splitting it into two giant half-moon nachos barely squeezing the greasy meat, cheese, and lettuce together.

The next thirty seconds are a **tornado chomping blur** as I bite fast to avoid the entire taco crumbling into a pathetic **beaver's dam** of splintered shells, sour cream smears, and grease drops. Usually it doesn't work and I'm left a pathetic mess with **bits of tomato in my hair** and a fine shell dusting on my pants.

That's why it's great if you actually manage to eat a taco without breaking it or anything falling out.

Because we didn't think you could do it.

And you proved us all wrong.

AWESOME!

The air just before a thunderstorm

Warm wind whips and whistles down the streets sending cigarette butts, crumpled receipts, and dry leaves swirling in all directions. Specks of dust glow in **orange sunbeam tints** as dark
clouds shuffle in the sky. There's a warm and steamy sense
of electric anticipation as lightning bolts **flash silently** in the
distance, dogs bark in the background, and everyone races for
cover.

Turning to your left you see two prune-faced old men sitting in overalls on wooden rocking chairs on the porch outside
the saloon. "Storm's a-coming," one offers and the other gives a
nearly imperceptible nod.

Next you hear the nylon swish of umbrellas popping open,
the scrape of **plastic chairs** dragging across patios, and feel the
adrenaline rushing through your veins just before the first big
boom.

Here come the jumbo drops.

AWESOME!

A perfectly sharp, pointy pencil

Most people look at a stack of pencils and pick the sharpest one. Don't you? Why is that? Is it because it lasts longer to write with or because it looks so nice and new?

I like the way sharp, pointy pencils feel when I write with them. It feels good. They also look nice and sharp. Some people say they are great because they look new and others say it's because when you write with one your writing **comes out smaller** than with a dull pencil. They're also good to draw with.

People even fight over pencils to get the pointiest one! What is it about sharp pencils? Always keep a sharpener with you to keep your pencils sharp!

Sharp, pointy pencils really are cool. No, wait! They're AWESOME!

—*Vina, age 12, California*

Any restaurant with old ladies doing the cooking

....

What's your favorite restaurant?

Mine is California Sandwiches, a tiny **hole-in-the-wall place** wedged between rusting clapboard houses in the middle of downtown Toronto. Sure, the word "sandwiches" is spelled wrong on the sign, the floor is always greasy, and the bathrooms may or may not have hot water, but the sandwiches are delicious, let me tell you that.

Old ladies wearing frilly aprons and **black glasses** pound bread and deep-fry pancake-sized chicken until it's brown, crispy, and dripping with hot oil. Then they place the pieces onto doughy buns the size of cabbages, pour a ladle of steaming tomato sauce on top, toss some cheese and mushrooms on there, and wrap it all inside **a mirrory foil** before handing it to you with fifty thin paper napkins and a grunt.

Last time I ate at California Sandwiches a skinny guy wearing a **backward cap** slowly walked between tables dragging two heavy black garbage bags. But Leslie and I barely noticed because we were eating our sandwiches like starved pigs over a trough of fresh slop. Twenty minutes later, our faces smeared in sauce, bellies bursting, belts unbuckled, we left with tired eyes and satisfied smiles.

I love California Sandwiches, but when I think about it, I love any restaurant with old ladies doing the cooking.

Old ladies have been here longer than anybody, and chances are they've been cooking for longer, too. Sure, I could probably order a pizza faster, but I'm no match when it comes to frying fish, **caramelizing onions**, or tossing a big circle of dough into the air before stretching it out with love.

Next time you bite into Dorothy's date squares from the bakery, **homemade meatballs** from Lucy's place, or slurp soup from that old lady's diner that's been at the side of the highway since before you were born, remember to stop and say thanks for the wisdom, thanks for the love, and thank you for the meal full of AWESOME!

Watching the sports highlights of the game you just finished watching

....

Couch potatoes of the world, hear my call.

We all know it's great capping off **three potato-chip-crumb-covered hours** on the sofa by watching the highlights of the game you just watched. Yes, you made it through all the time-outs, coaches' challenges, and pitching changes, so now's your chance to relive that hard-earned Sunday afternoon investment with a fast-motion reel of the best parts.

Also, it's fun comparing your **Sports Watching Skills** against the pros hunkered in the trailer outside the stadium. Did they show that blown call? That big save? Or that funny sign from the crowd? If they missed something big, just smile and chalk one up for potato.

Now, the best possible move is seeing the game live and then watching the highlights on your way home. You've got a lot more camera angles now and that added **Where's Waldo** pleasure of trying to find yourself cheering in the crowd.

You came, **you watched**, you saw the highlights.

AWESOME!

Singing the guitar solo

....

Never stop wailing.

When you're singing along with a song and the guitar solo suddenly starts up, it's time to keep *onnnnnn* going.

See, we can't have dead air in your **steamy morning shower** or the fans will just hear the sound of you soaping up your armpits and blowing your nose. Do you think they'll want an encore after that? And the screaming mosh pit in the backseat of your **Toyota Corolla** is just jumping for more. You better blast those high-pitched guitar notes or they'll go home cold and disappointed.

Never stop wailing.

When the words fade out and the guitar fades in, it's your big chance to keep the moment flowing.

You're already practiced from singing all the frontman and backup parts from the rest of the song. Now just add in the guitar solos your fingers can only dream of playing. Go from Axl to Slash in **"November Rain,"** start hitting high notes in "Bohemian Rhapsody," and, for good measure, feel free to vocalize the synthesizers in "Tainted Love."

"Sometimes I feel I've got to—boomp, boomp—run away. I've got to—boomp, boomp—get away."

Yes, you do have to get away—get away from the notion of your sing-a-long stopping when the guitar starts slashing, that is. People, when you've sung the first six minutes of **"Stairway**

to Heaven," there's no way you can disappoint the packed arena now. So step into the light at the front of the stage and shred that axe . . . verbally.

Also feel free to wobble your voice when stepping on your air distortion pedal, which may involve singing meows for all the notes. "Meow meEEOW meow meow meEEOW," you meow in a sweaty, head-banging daze.

Be one with the guitar solo.

Be one with the

AWESOME!

A sluggish internet signal picking up speed right before an important virtual meeting

—Robin Jenest Lezotte

Veering to avoid hitting a critter darting across the road and not killing it

—Cathleen Doyle Bernhardt

A steaming bald head after a satisfying winter run

—Graeme Drinkwalter

Hiking a favorite snow-covered trail and realizing those other tracks were from you and your dog two days earlier

—CJ Emerson

Getting the last blueberry lemon scone at the bakery

—Gay Wrye

Seamlessly and smoothly grabbing your credit card or license out of the wallet pocket on the first try without having to keep trying to grab it with the tips of your fingers

—Anna D'Alfonso

When the restaurant with the good pickles gives you extra pickles

—Sarahjane Cottrell

Moonlight snowshoeing with someone you love

—Carole Girard

When a six-part Excel formula works out correctly

—Ari Polsky

When sidewalks are clearing of snow and salt and you can ride your skateboard with your friends again

—Amber Rohal

When the Kleenex goes through the washer and dryer and miraculously stays in one piece

—Margaret Zimmerman

When you forget your library card but the librarian lets you pick up your holds anyway

—Krista Jorgensen

Successfully choosing the right lane at the car wash when it's super busy and getting in and out fast

—Megan Amos

Going out for lunch and your daughter is your server

—Tam Aiken

I used to love going to the grocery store when my daughter was working at the deli. She would say "I love you" when I left and I would just turn to the people around me and say "I love how friendly the staff is here!"

—Elizabeth Macdonald-Pratt

All the things you learned in third grade

....

What do you do?

I spent a lot of years working in offices but whenever I tried telling people about what I did their eyes always glossed over. "You lost me at spreadsheets," friends said while yawning and giving the waiter a head nod and ghost pour for another beer.

And I get that: jobs are complicated and narrow and it's getting hard to understand what anybody really does anymore.

When I was a kid I had a **big hardcover book** showing me all the things I could be when I grew up. "One day," it said, "you can be a teacher, factory worker, or astronaut! You can be a fireman, doctor, or traffic cop!" There was no mention of strategy consultants, event planners, or business analysts on special projects.

We all start down the same school path but along the way our lives take different turns. Highways curl into off-ramps, off-ramps split into side streets, side streets split into dirty paths every possible way until we all end up wherever we are today.

Life gets tricky and sometimes our day jobs feel so far away from everything we learned when we were young. I think that's why there's something so magical and sweet about the things we learned in third grade. Old enough and young enough to still be on the same path, this was when we all knew the same things:

1. **Types of Rocks.** Wasn't it mind-blowing to finally learn what we'd been crawling and walking on our whole lives? Igneous, sedimentary, and metamorphic were fun words for eight-year-olds to say over and over, too. Speaking of which, you remember what igneous was made of, right? Magma.

2. **How to Brush Your Teeth* (*and other hygiene basics).** Did you have those days when a nurse would come to school and teach everyone how to wash their bodies? Back in third grade my friend Natalie and I were setting up the bulletin board in the hallway when a nurse came to visit our class. We missed the entire visit and only heard apocryphal tales of oversized toothbrush sets and big plastic teeth. Most kids picked up the basics that day. Me, all I got was gingivitis.

3. **Cities and Countries and Planets.** Did you memorize all the states or provinces? Draw a map of your country in pencil-crayon? Did you slop papier-mache on a balloon and paint continents on it? Or draw a big chart of the planets? These early experiences gave us our first dizzying sense of place in this ever-expanding universe. Everything suddenly got smaller and bigger.

4. **Dinosaurs.** No offense to Marco Polo or the Boer War but learning about dinosaurs was the greatest history

lesson of all time. "Listen up kids," your teacher would say, trying to remain calm but clearly controlling his breathing, sitting cross-legged in cords on the carpet. "Before you got here, giant lizards *the size of houses* stomped around eating things right where you're sitting now. They all died when a huge meteor crashed into Earth . . . so heads up." Talk about a bombshell.

5. **Adding and subtracting.** Turns out nobody uses algebra, calculus, or geometry when they're older. It was all a ruse! "Hey Alan, can you trigonometry the wall to figure out where the studs are?" "Goretti, can you sine and cosine the expense reports?" Nobody's heard that before. Yes, I'm saying getting through life is **basic** math—adding up tabs at the bar, figuring out if you've got enough on your credit card for Christmas, and splitting bills with your roommates. Started back in third grade and still vital today.

6. **Storytelling.** When Mrs. Dorsman pulled her glasses down from her white poof of hair and headed for the rocking chair we all scrambled for a good spot on the dirty paper-thin green carpet lying over the tile floor. Suspense, funny voices, and chapter-ending cliff-hangers. Listening to a teacher tell a tale is an introduction to how we communicate, remember, and share.

The world sure was simpler back in third grade.

Hard facts and clear rules gave our lives solid edges and helped us color them in. Names of planets, types of triangles, and the boiling point of water added certainty in a fuzzy world.

The fuzziness comes back later, of course, when the edges of clarity are pulled up to reveal endless fuzziness underneath. We start realizing we don't know what's farther than far, why anything happens, or where we really even are.

Looking back and remembering all the things you learned in third grade is helpful stability in a dizzy, dizzy world.

AWESOME!

COMMENTS:

....

Casey says:

Third grade brought me roman numerals, math drills, and the starts of cursive. Seeing as I remember more of that than I remember things I'd learned in high school I'll have to agree with this page!

Ginny says:

My third grade teacher read novels to the class every afternoon for half an hour. We got to lay on pillows and relax and she even told us it didn't matter if we fell asleep. She said reading was just supposed to be relaxing and enjoyable. She taught me that reading was fun. I miss those days!

Simone says:

My third grade teacher was Mrs. White and she lived on an alpaca farm and brought alpaca wool into class to show us how soft it was.

Roz says:

I miss my DEAR time—Drop Everything And Read. It was always such a relaxing part to my day!

Laura says:

When I was in school, I LOVED when the nurse would come in and check for head lice . . . free head massage!!

Kathy says:

Mr. Kindon was terrific! We had so many incredible experiences: churning ice cream, tasting goat's milk directly from the goat he brought for a visit, having international meals to taste different foods, learning multiplication facts, listening as he read *The Wizard of Oz*, and practicing for our play. Great times with our farmer teacher!

> *Freddo replies:*
>
> You drank goat's milk DIRECTLY from a goat in third grade? That is a wild day in class! Hopefully in fourth grade they taught you guys about pasteurization?
>
> > *Kathy replies:*
> >
> > Well, he didn't exactly squirt it into our mouths but he did milk it and add chocolate to make chocolate goat's milk! All hail unsafe, reckless, germ-infested fun! We probably drank it right before going outside to play on all of the old, dangerous playground equipment.

The first time a new friend calls you by your nickname

....

Welcome to the inner circle.
   AWESOME!

Picking up your boyfriend's or girlfriend's sweater and suddenly smelling their smell

AWESOME!

Seeing a plane from another plane

Hello out there.

Staring out your airplane window and spotting another plane cruising calmly through salmon-and-clementine-colored clouds feels mysterious and magical. Open skies morph into traffic lanes from *The Jetsons* and it's almost jarring just how far we've come.

Scavenging bones, crossing ice bridges, rubbing sticks together, would we ever have guessed that one day we might spend a morning flying above the clouds in a comfortable chair staring out the window watching other people do the same thing?

AWESOME!

"I found out about this in *China Daily* and so the awesomeness is spreading quickly. When I started reading awesome things I immediately felt different. They were unlike anything I've ever heard or read before. And I was totally right. You will always have us seventh grade students in China reading, supporting, and agreeing with every one of these awesome things."

—Celine

"Greetings from Sweden! I am finding this book a wonderful oasis of love and nostalgia for a Swedish teacher in music. Thank you all for making my days rich and joyful."

—Linus

"I had my *Book of Awesome* sent to me from Montreal to Durban, South Africa, via Ethiopia and Johannesburg. It's a well-traveled book and I love it. I read it in front of Durban Stadium with the Atlantic and Pacific Oceans meeting the background!"

—Kim

Opening and sniffing a new pack of tennis balls

....

Not too many things that aren't cans of Coke sound like cans of Coke when they're opened. But tennis balls do, and that's part of their charm. Snap back the pop tab, enjoy that long *pshhhhh-hhhhhhh* sound, and then inhale a deep whiff of those vacuum-sealed, Korean-factory-packed, warm rubbery plastic fumes.

Tennis, anyone?

AWESOME!

COMMENTS:

....

Lane says:

"I think Pringles' initial intention was to make tennis balls. But on the day that the rubber was supposed to show up, a big truckload of potatoes arrived. But Pringles was a laid-back company. They said '**** it. Cut 'em up.' " —the late, great Mitch Hedberg

Peter says:

AAAAAHH! To an avid tennis player there is nothing like the smell of that just opened can of tennis balls. That bright green-yellow, that sound, that aroma. And the anticipation of the bounce and weight of new balls. What comes back is hours and hours and hours of hitting tennis balls, chasing tennis balls, watching tennis balls, loving the way that occasionally perfect stroke felt momentarily on my racket.

Nicole replies:

I love that stroke where it makes that perfect popping noise. I would play tennis for hours just to do that once.

Austin says:

OHHHHHHHHHHH that smell. We used to play baseball in the farmer's field by my house and weren't allowed to use real baseballs for fear of breaking his windows so used tennis balls instead.

Haley says:

Okay, you guys got me, I am going to head over to my local sports store right now just to buy a can and open them and smell them.

Successfully navigating your home in the dark

AWESOME!

Playing hide and seek with your kids but really you just hide and check your phone

....

In their youngest years children learn many things at incredible speed: how to walk, how to talk, how to hold a spoon, how to draw with a crayon. However, one thing they certainly do not learn is how to play hide and seek. Most children rank just below legally blind adults and golden retrievers when it comes to playing this timeless classic.

But that's a good thing! Why? Because it means playing hide and seek gives you a few minutes to secretly check your phone.

Here's how it works:

1. **Offer it up.** Ask your kids if they want to play hide and seek. Score major points with your partner for getting them out of the kitchen for a few minutes. They will want to be "it," which is perfect.
2. **Make the count.** Ask them to close their eyes and count to 30. Yes, 30. This will take them between five seconds and five minutes which is more than enough time to find a good hiding spot. (Note: Don't worry about being quiet while you look for a spot. Just remember to hide in a room with good signal.)

3. **Cozy is key.** For the actual spot, you don't want to be cramming yourself into the corner of a toys cupboard or sliding under a dusty bed. Ideally, you're going to be there for five to ten minutes, so try lying in your bed covered by a blanket, standing behind a door, or just sitting in the bathtub behind the curtain. Or just sit in the middle of the couch in the basement. This usually works because children do not like entering the basement.

4. **Screen time, dream time.** Once you're set, feel free to take out your phone and update your fantasy lineup, check some headlines, or bang out a few emails. Nothing wrong with posting a photo of you in the mirror peeking behind a shower curtain, either. "Loving a little hide and seek time with my little ones!" Hashtag best mom ever. Hashtag best dad ever. Hashtag family time.

5. **Finish the game.** Your kids will likely run straight to your partner so you need to establish up front that they won't squeal. Once you're done checking your phone you'll need to increasingly hint at your location. Knuckle-rap the wall, try some fake sneezing, and, if nothing else works just keep screaming, "I SAID I'M IN THE BASSSSSSEMENNNNNNT!!!" as loud as you can. You may need to provide turn-by-turn GPS directions.

Remember to act surprised and have a good laugh when your child finds you. If you need more phone time, just . . . play again! Never reverse roles unless you want your child hiding in plain view ten feet away from you.

Okay, you're ready, you're set, so what are you waiting for? Is your phone charged? You got it in your pocket? Are you ready to get in the game? Are you ready to get hashtag

AWESOME!

—*Michael Jones, Vancouver, British Columbia*

Actually winning one of those completely fixed carnival games

AWESOME!

Cracking open a brand new textbook

....

If you've been through the public school system you know that when it comes to textbooks you're getting worn-out, dog-eared hand-me-downs from decades past.

Tyrone from 1987, thank you for highlighting the entire Table of Contents. Melissa from 1999, we blame you for the somehow-still-getting-browner **mustard smear** in the index. And Juan, was it you in 2013 who managed to perfectly separate the book from its spine yet somehow keep it hanging together with a checkerboard of sticky threads?

This is why it's a beautiful moment when for once the teacher huffs and puffs into the room with a **heavy smooth cardboard box** and places it down at the front of the room. As she cracks it open and pulls out the first fresh textbook, you see clouds part, winds settle, and a sudden deep responsibility hitting you hard.

You go up to get your textbook and carry it back to your desk carefully. You look down at the crisp book and rub your fingers over the shiny cover before gently pulling it open. Notice how tight the book feels. Like it doesn't want to open yet and is using all its available faculties to stay shut as long as possible. It's a **pistachio nut** in a tight shell. It's an oyster that doesn't want to be shucked. It's a patient with a twisted neck who doesn't want to get on the chiropractor table.

Sniff those fresh printer fumes, feel the glossy pages on the

Table of Contents, and then shut it slowly to become one with the textbook. Now it's time to close your eyes and take a deep breath before the big moment.

Are you ready?

With one giant swoop, jab four fingers from either hand into the center of the book and yank it open with the loud ringing crack of dried binding glue shattering into a million little pieces of

AWESOME!

—*Lindsay Montgomery, United States*

Blowing bubbles in your milk

AWESOME!

Lazing on the couch after a big holiday feast

....

After getting stuffed with stuffing and **packed with potatoes** someone kindly rolls you to the couch and covers you with old blankets and leftover scraps of wrapping paper for your post-holiday meal snooze.

Smile sweetly and slowly fade into a spacey turkey high.

AWESOME!

Your first job

....

In my early 20s, I ran a sandwich shop.

Yes, I was a rootin', tootin', **mayo-squirting king** in the dirty mustard-smeared sandwich underbelly. I helped manage about a dozen high school kids and together we fired sandwiches down an assembly line, into paper bags, and right on out the door. I miss those long days full of dirty aprons, melted cheese, and unlimited refills.

Part of my job at the sandwich shop was conducting interviews. I ended up sitting down with a lot of teenagers who were applying for their first-ever job. They came in toting dog-eared resumes that looked like the Microsoft Word template, complete with skills like "Very punctual" and hobbies like "Insert hobbies here."

I kept a notepad along the way and here are some actual excerpts from interviews I conducted back then. Hold on to your hairnets, because we're going in:

> **ME:** So what did you end up doing when it got really busy at the sandwich place you used to work at?
>
> **HER:** Oh, it wasn't really a problem. We usually just locked the doors until we got through the lineup.
>
> **ME:** You locked the doors?
>
> **HER:** (*confused*) Yeah, but just until the line died down. We opened it up right after.
>
> **ME:** Oh. That's good.

HER: Also, another reason you should hire me is because I've always got along really well with people. Well, except for a few people.

ME: What did you do in those situations? How did you figure things out?

HER: Well, I was her manager, so I just forced her to wash dishes in the back so no one would see her. Then she quit.

ME: Oh. Okay.

HER: And the other woman I didn't like was really old.

ME: She was really old?

HER: Yeah. Way too old. Really old.

ME: Okay.

ME: Do you have a way to get to work?

HER: Well, I don't have a car. But I might be able to take my sister's car.

ME: Okay, cool. That's not a problem?

HER: No. My sister's boyfriend just . . . Well, I don't want to talk about it. My sister's boyfriend just did something . . . and now she's going to the East Coast . . . so I can probably get her car.

ME: Neat.

ME: What's something you liked and didn't like about your last job?

HER: I liked it because everyone was nice.

ME: What did they do?

HER: They were really nice.

ME: Okay. Was there anything you didn't like about it?

HER: Some of the people weren't that nice.

ME: So they weren't all nice?

HER: No. I guess some were nice. Some weren't nice.

ME: So do you have any questions about the restaurant?

HIM: Yeah. Do you have an assorted sub?

ME: An assorted sub? Yeah. There are two different types of assorted subs.

HIM: Cool. What's on the first one?

ME: Well, it's an Italian so it's got salami, pepperoni, and ham.

HIM: What about cheese?

ME: Yeah, there's mozzarella.

HIM: Sauce?

ME: Sauce? Oh, yeah, there's vinaigrette on there. And it has tomatoes, onions, lettuce, and black olives, too.

HIM: Hmm . . . What's on your steak sub?

(*10 more minutes of him quizzing me on subs for no apparent reason*)

ME: So grab whatever you want. Lunch is on me. Then we'll sit down and talk for a few minutes.

HIM: I'll have a turkey sub.

TEENAGER BEHIND COUNTER: What size would you like?

HIM: The biggest one.

TEENAGER BEHIND COUNTER: Sure, anything else?

HIM: Large Coke.

TEENAGER BEHIND COUNTER: Sure, anything else?

HIM: Can I get a big cookie?

TEENAGER BEHIND COUNTER: Sure, anything else?

HIM: *(looking at menu)* Umm . . .

ME: *(laughing)* Do you eat at home?

HIM: Yes.

ME: *(laughing)*

HIM: *(deadpan)*

ME: *(deadpan)*

HIM: *(deadpan)*

ME: So tell me about some of your hobbies.

HER: *(10-second pause)* Um . . . *(giggles)*

ME: Something you do after school?

HER: *(lightbulb going off)* Um, messaging?!

ME: Oh, yeah, messaging?

HER: Yeah! I like chatting with my friends.

ME: That's cool. Is there anything else you do for fun? On any school teams or clubs?

HER: *(10-second pause)* Um . . . hanging out?

ME: Hanging out?

HER: *(trying to explain it to me)* Hanging out with friends?

ME: Right. Hanging out with friends.

HER: *(happy I understand)* Yeah!

ME: I'm going to give you a situation and I'd like to see how you think about it when you tell me what you would do, okay?

HER: Okay.

ME: Okay. You're working the cash register. Suddenly a woman comes up to you holding a piece of plastic and complains that she found the plastic in her sandwich. She says to you that you broke her tooth and owe her a thousand dollars. What would you do?

HER: (*scared face*)

ME: It's okay. There's no right or wrong answer. Take your time.

(*30 seconds pass*)

HER: (*holding scared face*)

ME: It's okay. Don't worry. Take your time to think about it.

(*30 seconds pass*)

HER: Um, okay. I'm ready.

ME: Okay. What would you do?

HER: I'd give her the money.

ME: You'd give her a thousand dollars from the till?

HER: (*realizing that probably sounds bad*) Oh . . . uh, no! (*long pause*) I mean I'd give her my PERSONAL money.

ME: You'd give her a thousand dollars from your wallet?

HER: Yes.

(*10 seconds of us staring at each other and blinking*)

ME: Can you tell me about a problem you had while working with a group and how you resolved that problem?

HER: Um . . . (*giggle*)

ME: It's okay. Take your time.

HER: Okay. (*30 seconds pass*) Okay, one time in marketing class I didn't like my group so I did something else.

ME: You mean you left the group?

HER: Yeah. I asked the teacher if I could leave the group and she said yes. So I did a report or something.

ME: Oh, okay. And how did the rest of the group feel about it?

HER: I don't know. They all stopped talking to me.

ME: Oh . . . okay. Well, what didn't you like about working with them?

HER: They were just ignorant.

ME: Can you tell me more about the project?

HER: Well, we had to make up a product and then advertise it. And we got cereal. But they wanted to make a cereal that was made out of rocks.

ME: Rocks?

HER: Yeah, I know. That's why I left the group.

ME: They wanted to make a cereal out of rocks?

HER: Yeah.

ME: So you said you took marketing. What's something you think we could do to help advertise the shop?

HER: (*30-second pause, then a worried look*)

ME: It's okay. There's no right or wrong answer. I'm just interested to see what you'd do to advertise.

HER: (*nods, then another 30 seconds pass*) Um, okay, I'm ready.

ME: Okay.

HER: I think you should do a whole bunch of TV ads?

ME: In this city?

HER: Yeah.

ME: Okay, okay, cool idea. What do you think that would cost?

HER: I don't know. Probably a million dollars?

ME: How do you like your high school?

HER: It's okay, but the teachers don't like the kids. They think they know everything but they don't. And all the kids are ignorant.

ME: Really? What are they ignorant about?

HER: Everything.

ME: (*laughing*) You mean because they think that a good breakfast cereal would be one with rocks in it?

HER: (*confused look*)

Well, honest and eager, we all once walked into our first job interview sweating buckets, too. But if somebody was kind to us we learned a lot, grew a lot, and eventually one day we got busy working.

So let's stop for a moment today and remember that everything we know about work started way back on that very first job. Whether it was flipping burgers, babysitting kids, or washing cars, all those experiences added up to getting right where we are. Growing on the job, making office pals, and making a difference are all things worth respecting.

Let's say thanks to the job that started it all.

AWESOME!

When the videoconference chat fills up with compliments about the thing you just said in the meeting

....

We have official written proof of your brilliance.
   Remember to take a screenshot.
   AWESOME!

Finally taking your mask off after wearing it for hours

....

It just feels like freedom.
   AWESOME!

Any bite where there's more chocolate than cookie in the chocolate chip cookie

AWESOME!

When you clink every single glass for cheers even if it means getting up and walking around the restaurant table

Forget that tilting glass and head nod from a distance garbage.
    We're talking about the real deal.
    AWESOME!

Anything that can grow wings

··

When I was a kid we had one metal garbage can.

It was the kind **Oscar the Grouch** lived in and on garbage days my sister and I walked to school passing the same metal garbage cans at the end of every driveway.

One day as we were growing up, the clouds parted and blue recycling bins were born and then, many years later, bugles blared and green compost bins were launched. I remember getting a brand new green bin on the foot of my driveway at my first-ever house which included a helpful note from the city telling me to feel free to load it up with moldy compost each week—eggshells, stale bread, raw chicken, paper towel.

In the beginning I had no problem with green-binning. It was stinky, sure, but a small price for diverting a pail full of garbage from the dump each week. If somebody was willing to drive around town and pick up our chicken bones and the fuzzy chili from the back of the fridge, then hey, who were we to stop them? We began using new biodegradable green bags until the city left us stickers telling us that those bags didn't degrade very well so we should just dump our compost in the bin **au naturel**. We said sure, kept doing what we were doing, and in general felt smug and proud of ourselves.

Then the maggots came.

I guess the blazing summer heat did a number on the rotten food sitting in the green bin because one morning I opened the lid to awaken a wall full of white, squirmy maggots that were **wriggling up the side** and **all over the lid**. Stunned, I took a step back, threw my hands in the air, let out a high-pitched scream, and ran to my car.

I drove to work hoping it was all a dream.

When I got there I told my coworker Laurie about the harrowing experience. "Oh, yeah, that happens," she said nonchalantly, not even looking up from her screen, her long fingernails clacking away. "We call it the **Maggot Wagon** at our house. But don't worry! They'll just fly away eventually."

Fly away eventually?

Well, I did a bit of research and discovered I was evidently last to learn about this whole metamorphosis thing. Turns out maggots are just **baby flies**—cute little larval worms looking to grow some wings and fly around until they fall in love and make some baby maggots on their own. It's almost cute.

Caterpillars? Same thing. After wriggling up tree trunks and nibbling on leaves for a while, they finally clue in and make their own chrysalis, where they dissolve their entire body into a liquid goop, and then, yes, **grow wings**, reemerging as beautiful butterflies, haphazardly fluttering off into the setting sun.

Growing wings sounds like an extremely tough job. First you need to spin yourself a cocoon, chrysalis, or hide in a tree knot or something. Then I imagine there's a lot of gritting your teeth, squeezing all your muscles really tight, and screaming, "NNNNNNN! NNNNNNNN! NNNNNNNN!" a lot. Plus, you're on your own. No one's there to cheer you on, wipe your brow, or hand you a paper cup of Gatorade. You just push and push and push and push until you finally give birth . . . to yourself.

When I ran away from those maggots I was heeding emotions and emotions only. They freaked out so I freaked out and that left no room to look closer. Nature is beautiful even when it looks ugly and we get to decide, we get to decide, when we might pause to look a little deeper instead.

AWESOME!

When your kid falls asleep on you

It doesn't matter how old. It doesn't matter where. An infant on your chest, right home from the hospital. Your toddler in their bed, drifting off in the middle of a book. Asleep in your arms while you carry them. Crawling into your bed. Leaning on your shoulder on an airplane.

Because they had such a great day. **Because they're sick.** Because they trust you and love you and you're spending time together.

AWESOME!

—*Ryan Holiday, Austin, Texas*

Finally cutting off that overgrown big toenail

....

Big toes are tough.

Chances are good your big toe has the largest nail you've got. And if you're anything like me you don't quite realize it needs chopping until you pop a hole in your socks and look down one day to discover you've grown scraggly **Hobbit Feet** complete with dirty and jagged **Forest Toenails**.

That's why it's so satisfying to saw it off.

There are a few ways to get the job done:

- **The Big Clip.** My brother-in-law Dee pulls out this fancy salon kit he has that contains a Jumbo Nail Clipper. Have you seen one of these things? They're enormous and well-suited to the task of slicing off the big mighty toenail. Clip, clip, you're done. And you can use it to trim the hedges afterwards.
- **Temporary Fang Nail.** This is where you clip both the left and right sides of the nail first but then end up with a temporary sharp and jagged fang nail sticking out like a dagger. This is the closest you're getting to wolverine claws so enjoy it for a few minutes. Slice open a garbage bag, climb a tall pine tree, or leap on an unsuspecting grizzly.

- **The Slow and Steady.** The classic. Pull out nail scissors or a small rusty clipper somebody bought from the dollar store ten years ago. Set your foot on the bathroom counter and scrunch your eyebrows while slowly clip-clip-clipping your way across. Important note: Finish! Don't get hasty and try ripping the last bit because that may cause a wild and unpredictable line you'll have to stare at for the next two weeks.

Now, when you're done you have a freshly shorn toe and one massive toenail. Does it gross you out? It shouldn't! It's part of your magical human body. No toenail guilt, no toenail shame here. In fact, I suggest before you toss it in the trash you pause and lift that majestic nail into the setting sun and for one beautiful moment just smile and think . . .

AWESOME!

Watching seniors do water aerobics

Speedos snapped on and earplugs pushed in, a group of old folks carefully climb down the ladder into the local pool for some submerged cardio. And if you happen to catch a glimpse of the jumping jacks and karate punches, then you know how fun it is to see all the **wet perms**, dripping glasses, and smiling faces.

They just look so happy.

AWESOME!

Getting into your parked car at the same time as the guy gets into his parked car next to you and instead of racing to see who's faster to leave you get the head nod for you to go first

—Maureen Schlosser

Going into the women's public bathroom in the morning and seeing the seat up and knowing no one has sat there since it's been cleaned

—Sonya Shaffer

Ah yes, the honor of being the first butt of the day

—Stella Stokes

Panicking to prep a meeting agenda and then finding out you drafted one weeks ago

—Catherine Joyes

When your book club decides to read a cookbook one month and everybody brings something they made from the cookbook so the book club discussion is both fun and delicious

—Veronica Jerguna

The moment when the airplane boarding is complete and the seat next to you is still empty

—Leah Boothe

When the person who banged your car in the parking lot leaves a note with their number

—Jason Hopgood

Hearing one roofer say to the other roofer, "We're almost done" after three straight days of hammering above your head while you work from home

—Lesley Diane

Dang how big is that roof over ya head? Texas we get it done in one day

—Martin Groseclose

That plot moment in a novel that makes you go ohhhhhhhhh

—Heather Morse

And the moment when the title of the book reveals itself!

—Robin Lezotte

When you're driving really slowly and the address you're looking for is actually visible from the road

—Haley Ingram

Wheelchair accessible nature trails

—Paige Perry

Yessssss!!! I'm a chair user myself and they are so hard to come by!!!!

—Chelsea Perry

When the baby wakes up right before you need to leave the house so you don't have to wake them up

—Pam Hansen

Biting into an apple that looks spongy and discovering that it's actually crisp

—Susan Drake

Seeing all the dogs in car backseats coming through the drive-through at my job

—Shi Lovell

When emergency response vehicles are coming down the road and all the drivers on both sides of the road pull over right away

—Megan Amos

Hearing the little boys playing and laughing upstairs from my basement apartment

—Charlene Owen

Approaching another car in the dark on a deserted road and you both politely turn off your high beams the exact same millisecond

—Amy Biagini

A fresh set of contact lenses

—Neil Hopkins

Yes, and how crisply defined everything becomes again when you get your new glasses

—Jane Slater

Cutting your sandwich into triangles

Welcome back to Childhood.

Gooey grilled cheese drips and oozes onto plastic dishes on **wobbly kitchen tables**. Dusty sunlight beams down on the dog as you sit with your brother on Saturday afternoon beside the whirring fridge with rainbow letter magnets in front of the **pea-green stove**.

Sandwich triangles give us more first bites and let us chomp right into the **taste nucleus** of our lunch.

Welcome to Flavor Country, everybody.

We're home.

AWESOME!

Letting the waves bury your feet at the beach

Stare into the sparkling ocean distance as your feet slowly sink into the wet sand at the edge of the waves. Rub your palms on the sand for a **million little massages** as your mind stares deeply into the setting sun in the distance. Pink and purple streaks color the sky as you breathe in warm and salty ocean winds and squish-slide your feet deeper and deeper and deeper while closing your eyes and letting your mind fluttery-fly away . . .

AWESOME!

When a stranger laughs at a joke between you and your friends

···

Suddenly your private one-liner is granted objective joke-telling credibility.

Way to slay the coffee shop lineup, **crack up the ladies behind the sandwich counter**, or leave the old guys at the bus station urinals in stitches.

Way to get everybody laughing.

Way to get everybody feeling

AWESOME!

Homemade food on the potluck table

Get lost, Oreos.

Who wants to pull out that crinkly plastic tray when we've got a plate of Eileen's famous chocolate-coconut squares right beside them? Suresh's deviled eggs, Lee Tam's spicy wings, and even the boss's homemade brownies from a box are what we're really after here.

Keep your wet shrimp rings, **unopened boxes of granola bars**, and neon-green mini-cupcakes.

Homemade food on the potluck table is a sign of investment, a sign of spending time, and a sign of giving and receiving love in the form of heaping piles on paper plates.

AWESOME!

The first time you get to ride in the front seat of the car

....

You waited a long time.

Cruising backward in the baby seat, strapped into the **clunky toddler chair**, sharing the bench with your brother, you spent years putting up with child locks, unopenable windows, and bad views.

When you finally ride in the front seat you deserve congratulations.

You just got promoted to adult.

AWESOME!

Completely guessing the right answer on a multiple choice test

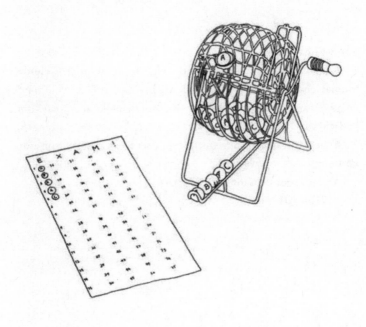

AWESOME!

The Surprise Left Turn Arrow

Has a long left turn lane got you down?

Are you backed up past where the lane even begins?

Is there an **18-wheeler** in front of you pulling a wraparound turn at the speed of sloth?

Did the guy in front of you just hit the brakes when you expected him to gun it, which froze you behind the line for another light?

Did a car going the other way run a red which kept you stranded in no-man's-land?

Well, if you're **stalled at the amber** and feeling red, we've got just the cure for you:

The Surprise Left Turn Arrow.

When that surprise neon-green arrow flashes it's like a curtain rises, an audience cheers, and the stage is just begging you on.

AWESOME!

Not bumping your head on that thing you always bump your head on

Nice try, metal trunk latch.
    Almost got me, airplane overhead bin.
    Maybe next time, hanging basement lightbulb.
    AWESOME!

That person who brings treats into work on Friday

Do you work in an office where a Business Casual Hero brings treats for everyone on Fridays?

It usually goes down a few ways:

Level 1: Email Scrambles. A mass email is sent out reading "If anyone wants leftover brownies, come to Debbie's desk NOW!!!"

Level 2: Treat Fairies. This is the plate of blueberry and cheese danishes someone kindly left on the hallway filing cabinet. All melted and stuck together from sitting out for six hours? Yes. Still edible? Absolutely.

Level 3: Post-Vacation Sugar Nation. This is a little plastic bag of exotic cartoon-cat-themed jellies from the guy who just got back from Tokyo.

Level 4: Three-way tie between Girl Scout Cookie Scattering, Post-Halloween Chocolate Dump, and After-Easter Eggathon.

Level 5: Homemade Holiday Treatery. When Christmas is coming, the vice president brings two tins of her husband's famous shortbread or the new secretary brings their drool-worthy date squares.

Yes, there are so many ways to get the treats going and the **office flowing** for the Friday night Funrise.

So let's stop and high five those heroes bringing treats to pump us up for the weekend.

AWESOME!

The "access granted" noise of your hotel room door unlocking even after it was touching your phone

....

It is late. It is late, and you've had the world's longest day, like "eleven hours of mind-numbing meetings" long, or "Disney World with two toddlers" long, or "full day of conference small-talk with strangers" long. You stumble into the lobby of your hotel, limping slightly due to a terribly ill-conceived footwear choice. You're starving and it suddenly dawns on you that all you've consumed today is a **blueberry scone** sometime in the before-lunch haze.

All you can think about is the sweet relief of your hotel room: crisp, clean sheets. A responsive thermostat. *Room service*. You hobble through the lobby and find the elevators. Your bag weighs twelve thousand pounds. In the elevator, you push the button for your floor as you lean against the wall, digging through your pockets for your room key.

You're still fumbling with one hand looking for the key as the doors open and you step out into the hallway. Success! Your fingers close around your key card, and a split second later, your heart sinks: **it was right next to your phone**. Uh oh. Will it still work? Did it get deactivated? Will this be one of those times you make it all the way down the long hallway to your room only to be met with a blinking red light and the reality of being required to walk seventeen miles back down to the lobby, stand in a line, talk to a person, and then do all of this again?

These thoughts consume you as you close in on your room, which is the farthest one from the elevator. **Might as well be in Cleveland.** A prayer runs through your mind: please work. please work. pleasework. pleasework. pleasework.

Finally, you arrive at your door. Your bed is so close you can taste it. Gingerly, you dip the key card into the slot. *Pleasework.*

The light flashes green. You hear a mechanical "something is happening" noise. You turn the door handle and it opens, seamlessly, into your hotel room.

AWESOME!

—*Emily McDowell, Portland, Oregon*

Helping out an insect struggling to do something

....

Picture this:

You're biking down leaf-slicked side streets when your wheel slips and you fly over the handlebars before crashing onto the road. You smack it hard and are lying on your side in a mess of bike chains and bleeding legs.

But then, out of nowhere, a giant hand reaches down and yanks you up by the collar, setting you back on your feet. Then the hand **zooms away** and you're standing on the side of the road dazed, confused, and happy.

That's what I picture it felt like for the wiggling upside-down beetle I flipped over the other day.

Next time you release a fly from its **Between-Sliding-Doors Prison**, let a frantic ladybug in a swimming pool crawl onto your finger and fly away, or help a bumblebee banging its head against your window buzz out the door, stop to enjoy the moment of helping out a fellow living thing.

We're all sharing the same planet, we're all sharing the same sun, and it's great helping an insect do something, so it can get its doing something done.

AWESOME!

Getting a glimpse of the first parade float coming around the corner

AWESOME!

Seeing a big dog sitting in the driver's seat of a parked car

....

What was your worst job ever?

I was telling a couple friends that unclogging grease traps with my bare hands was at the top of my list. Pulling open that **rusty black box** from under the triple sink at the back of the restaurant released a foul **Rotting Meat Scraps Fom Six Months Ago** stench that is forever seared in my brain.

My friend Scott said that was nothing compared to cleaning out the urinals at the rowdy bar he worked at in high school. Being the low man on the grill meant the boss would hand him a roll of paper towels with an apologetic pat on the back at closing time.

I thought Scott won but then Tyler dared suggest collecting shopping carts at the grocery store parking lot was worse. We scoffed in disbelief, but he launched into it:

"Just think about it," Tyler said. "You're outside. Start with that. Both your jobs were inside. And now you're on a never ending search for lost carts—never ending!—which you have to snap all together before pushing the world's heaviest **Cart Train** back inside without bumping into anything. Snow, slush, rain, doesn't matter. You freeze for hours all by yourself. And the carts never stop." His eyes started tearing up as he stared at the empty pizza box in front of us. "They just never stop."

It was a good argument but after a serious three-second deliberation we decided to rule Tyler's job out. Why? The jury argued **Cart-Picker-Upper** gets fresh air, good exercise, and the added bonus of laughing out loud whenever he sees a big dog sitting in the driver's seat of that parked car with the windows down.

Yes, he gets to imagine that dog trying to figure out how to drive in case some **killer disease** wipes out the entire human population while his owner grabs bananas. "It's up to dogs now," you can hear him thinking, gamely pawing the slippery steering wheel, staring at you with sad, tired eyes. "Don't just look at me . . . Where's the stupid emergency brake?"

Seeing a big dog sitting in the driver's seat of a parked car with the windows down ranks up there with pink sunrises over glittery oceans, old people holding hands, or videos of laughing babies. A big dog in a driver's seat is the car equivalent of a **Friendly Pet Welcome** at your front door.

Whether it's pushing carts through snow and seeing adorable big dog faces, mopping **dusty school hallways** and catching little kid embraces, or spilling coffee in turbulence before landing in sandy new places . . . well, every terrible job really has silver linings, quiet pleasures, and hidden little moments of
AWESOME!

Sitting in the very back row of a sporting event

You are never really sure what **Section 409, Row U** means until you climb and climb and climb, clutching your ticket and wondering why you didn't hire a Sherpa back at base camp.

But then you discover you're in the last row and are suddenly elated because you know the last row is far better than the rows in front of it. You can stand up, post your sign on the concrete wall, and enjoy a **bird's-eye view** of the entire field.

Does anyone remember sitting at the far end of the right field bleachers at Exhibition Stadium? It was as far away from the outfield fence as the outfield fence was from home plate.

Nothing better than arguing balls and strikes from there. AWESOME!

—*Mike Dover, Etobicoke, Ontario*

That one really weird food combination that only you love

AWESOME!

Your skin

....

You arrived gift-wrapped.

When you came into the world you had many incredible organs inside, but your whole body was wrapped in the biggest of them all.

Let's pause to count five reasons why your skin deserves some praise:

1. **Your body's bouncer.** Your skin has three layers: the epidermis, the dermis, and subcutaneous fat. The epidermis is on top and is part of your body's security system acting like a club bouncer sending underage dirt and low-class bacteria down the street. Tough bouncers in dark glasses mean no dirty trespasses, but the job sadly leads to burnout and high turnover. You lose over thirty thousand skin cells every minute of every day, which adds up to nine pounds of dead skin falling off your body each year. Thank goodness new cells are always forming below the surface.

2. **Built-in thermostat.** Your epidermis is also full of sweat glands, which act like your body's thermostat. If you get hot running around, your body sends warm blood closer to the surface to cool off—causing classic Red Face. And, at the same time, your skin releases sweat, which evaporates and helps you cool down.

But what if you're cold? Don't worry! Now your skin pushes blood cells down to create goose bumps, which pull your hairs up and create little warm air pockets. And, as if that's not enough, it also produces more oil to coat your skin and help keep heat in. Did I mention the monthly cost for this always-on heating and air-conditioning service? Nothing!

3. **World's fastest note passing.** We live in wild ways with texts speeding across the planet in seconds. But beaming satellites have nothing on your dermis, which contain nerve endings that speed-dial your brain whenever you touch anything. Grandma hair, cantaloupe rind, or someone else's lips—there's a wonderfully sensitive near-instant connection between dermis, heart, and mind. So next time you run your fingertips across a loved one's hands, remember to thank your dermis for amplifying the power of touch.

4. **Waterproof or bust.** Your dermis is also home to glands that endlessly squeeze out oil to keep your skin lubricated and waterproof. Forgot your rubber boots for that muddy walk through the woods? Don't worry! Those puddles won't keep you wet for long.

5. **Safety shocks.** There's a reason the third layer of skin is called subcutaneous fat. Yes, it's full of fat to help your body stay warm and absorb shocks. Ever have a massive wipeout on a slick patch of ice? Did you end up with a big yellow and purple bruise rather than a shattered pelvis? Just thank the subcutaneous junk in your trunk.

Liver, large intestine, small intestine, and brain, we know you're important. You're our next four largest organs! But while you hide inside, there is one organ on the front lines taking care of you today, tomorrow, and for all the days to come.

So thank you, skin.

From everyone.

AWESOME!

"My awesome? Besides working close enough to Lake Michigan that I can spend lunch there? When after a long night out at the bar with friends and you are sound asleep but then suddenly you bolt upright with panic! Did you grab your credit card from the bar? Did you leave your phone in the car? You scramble out of bed and check your pants, hoodie, and purse until you find everything and then sink right back into a stress-free sleep. All before waking up and going to the beach later. AWESOME!"

—Jess, Chicago, Illinois

Talking to little kids about what they want to be when they grow up

Leslie is an elementary school teacher.

For years we loved swapping stories after work because we were doing such different things. I came home from an office job in the suburbs and told horror stories about **yellow-font-on-white-background** PowerPoint slides while she would tell me about teaching kindergartners how to tie their shoes.

One day she asked her students what they wanted to be when they grew up.

One boy wanted to be a veterinarian, one girl wanted to be a scientist, and then a shy girl got all excited, **her eyes lit up**, and she waved both arms in the sky.

"Tandy, what do you want to be?" Leslie asked.

"Oh, oh, oh!!! I want to be a farm!!!"

Now, Leslie didn't want to kill the kid's creativity despite the challenges of metamorphizing into a few hundred acres of **soybean plantations** so she just softly challenged back a bit to see where she could lead the conversation.

"Tandy, I love farms, too! There's horses and barns and trucks! There are people driving tractors, people milking cows, and people feeding chickens. Do you want to be one of those people?"

Tandy scrunched her tiny nose like a pig before looking up in a head-twisty daze.

Leslie tried again.

"It's hard to be a farm because a farm is a *place*," she explained. "You could be a farmer though."

Tandy shook her head back and forth. Definitely didn't want to be a farmer. She put her head in her hands for a few seconds before getting really, really excited again. Her mouth dropped open, **her eyeballs popped wide**, and she started flapping her arms like wings.

She looked up at Leslie with skyrocketing energy and the force of a thousand trains before jumping off the carpet and yelling out:

"Oh, oh, oh!!! I want to be a pumpkin!!!"

AWESOME!

The Superfast Group Cleanup

....

Everybody loves turkey dinner.

Nobody loves the massive spread of crusty dishes, **gravy boats**, and sticky-smeared cutlery afterwards. You can almost hear a tuba farting slowly down the octave as the camera pans across the counter.

Some poor soul's night is officially . . . over.

But that's when a **Superfast Group Cleanup** can suddenly appear and helpfully make all those problems just disappear.

Grab one of these jobs and work at double time for ten minutes to get it done:

1. **The Table Clearer.** Are you good at Jenga? How about making giant piles of dirty laundry not fall over? If so, you are the perfect Table Clearer. Your job is piling all the plates as high as possible, while constantly moving dirty knives, forks, and scraps of food to the top. Another important skill is delivering your dirty dishes to The Dishwasher at a good pace. Too fast and the counter gets crammed. Too slow and it's time for a new career.

2. **The Dishwasher.** This sudsy someone needs to have a well-established Dishwashing Plan. Are we going soapy-rinsy with two full sinks? Or are we more of a constantly running the faucet power washer? The

important thing is that the dishes are clean and move quickly to Dryer Guy. The Dishwasher must be speedy but keep an eye out for quality. It takes a long time to build trust in this gig and only one half-chewed kernel of corn stuck to the bottom of a plate to lose it.

3. **The Putter-Awayer.** Salt, pepper, ketchup, we've got a home for you. The Putter-Awayer works in tandem with The Table Clearer to get everything back to the fridge or cupboards. Please note: The Putter-Awayer has the steepest learning curve of any job because it includes tasks both easy (putting ketchup in the fridge), medium (quickly rearranging all the half-used salad dressings on the fridge door so another one squeezes in), and advanced (correctly figuring out the right Tupperware container for leftovers and then actually finding the lid). A Bachelors of Geometry is recommended.

4. **Dryer Guy.** Sorry, but this is the loser job. If The CEO throws a tea towel at your face and tells you to dry dishes they're saying, "We don't trust you with anything else." The proof is that your entire job can be made obsolete by just leaving the dishes on the rack for an hour.

5. **The CEO.** The humble servant leader of the group. They help people choose tasks, put the music on, direct traffic flow, and relieve bottlenecks. They do all the small jobs that don't get noticed like getting a new garbage bag, wiping up any spills, and giving

everyone a firm handshake afterwards. The CEO must have a deep understanding of all roles so they can jump in if anybody suddenly goes to the bathroom to check their phone.

Yes, the Superfast Group Cleanup (SFGC) after the big holiday dinner makes messy kitchens disappear in minutes. A ballet of sweat socks, **tea towels**, and gently clinking plates thrills children watching from the linoleum floor and old folks sitting in the next room under dim dining room chandeliers.

Now let's get back to the party.

AWESOME!

Sending yourself emails to do stuff in the future

....

It's good getting along with Future You.

Whether it's all-caps screaming to pick up the milk, terse finger-wagging emojis reminding you to go to the gym, or polite memos to your Personal Self from your Work Self, the point is you're making real plans to get the job done.

Variations on the theme include The Time-Delayed Send, **The Bizarro Self Voicemail**, or the classic 10 Exclamation Mark Morning Surprise.

You have one new message.

AWESOME!

Somehow waking up at the right time even though you forgot to set your alarm

....

Close call.

Last night you hit the pillow without a safety net and fell into a free-falling slumber with no backup plan. You could have slept all day but somehow you sprang up like a **jack-in-the-box** in the morning and stared in confusion at your curiously quiet clock.

When you see that you woke up at the right time be sure to tap your temple with your finger and smile slowly at the genius of your own brain.

Thank goodness your subconscious stayed up all night counting seconds so it could pop you up right when you needed.

AWESOME!

Spotting a cat in an apartment window

Finding a little stack of old photographs when cleaning the
house and pausing time to briefly flip through the memories

Cracking your back by twisting using your desk chair

When your grandparents sneak you money

Taking a shower under the rainspout at the cottage naked

Finally letting that fart out you have been
holding for the whole first date

Driving around a parking lot looking for an open space
and someone parked right in front of you leaves

Racing to catch a closing elevator door and suddenly
seeing someone's arm stick out and open it

Reading a whole book cover to cover in one go

Opening windows for the first time to let the air enter after the
winter season and smelling spring air and hearing bird sounds

Looking at the reflection of the Moon on a lake
at midnight when it's quiet around and you can
just hear insects and the sounds of waves

Licking the powdered cheese off your fingers

Feeling your girlfriend squeezing your hand
while watching a good scary movie

Walking into the classroom right as the bell rings

First swipe of the lip balm

Petting a warm cat after playing in the snow

The feeling you get as soon as you get off a trampoline

The sound of a metal bat hitting a baseball really hard

That feeling of relief just after taking off a pair of hockey skates

Seeing an animal-crossing sign for a type of animal
you've never seen on an animal-crossing sign

Becoming friends with the crossing guard

Accidentally cooking the pasta perfectly al dente

Pencil-end erasers that actually work

When a song by your favorite band
unexpectedly plays in a public place

Falling asleep on the couch in the middle of the day
to a crackling fire when it's snowing outside

Bringing the best dish to the potluck

Catching a pesky mosquito with one hand

When the printer has the exact amount of paper
left in it for the thing you're printing

Watching people learn to hula-hoop

Watching little kids eat ice cream on a hot day

When the umpire falls over at the ball game

Very slowly putting your hand into a deep bag full of flour

Coming home from being at the beach all day
and still smelling like sun, sand, and lotion

When the clothes you wore back in high school come back into style

Shampoo mohawks

When the word you spell wrong by like five letters
somehow gets fixed by autocorrect

Having done your homework the one day
a really strict teacher checks it

Hugging people who smell good

Acing a test without studying

Finding another roll of toilet paper sitting behind
you on the tank just when you need it

The sound of the ice cream truck getting louder and louder

No longer listening to the sound of hands thrashing through
LEGO bins all day when your kids go back to school

The hilarious growl of a very tiny puppy attempting to be tough

Crispy fried cheddar from the edge of the grilled cheese sandwich

The booming and groaning made by frozen
lakes on extremely cold nights

When the elevator in your apartment building goes directly from
the parking level to your floor without stopping in the lobby

Mastering chopsticks

Watching little drops of rain race across your car window

When the Zamboni drives over that last
little snowy triangle on the rink

Making sure nobody's looking and then scratching your armpit

When you flirt with that cute bartender and they flirt back

Getting up on the rooftop of a farmhouse and catching the full
moon crest the horizon on a perfectly clear and calm night

Getting 21 nuggets when you ordered 20 at McDonald's

When the company that laid you off calls you
back up to hire you for a more senior job

Rolling up the yoga mat perfectly on the first try

When the neighbor leaves a bag of crab apples on
your porch so you can make a batch of jelly

Flying over mountains

Have you ever ruled a planet?

Me, no—but I've wanted to! **Wouldn't it be fun?** We could all have our own. We'd be like celebrities buying up tiny islands in the ocean. Just with planets in the middle of the universe.

It doesn't happen often, but when I fly over mountains in an airplane I feel like the **Ruler of Earth**. Zooming through darkening blue skies, I look down at my rocky vistas and **snowcapped peaks** in wonder. Frost freckles the window and clouds blur my view, but nothing keeps me from staring into the icy abyss below.

It's trippy letting your brain slip into endless questions: How long have the mountains been there? How did they get there? How many places like this are there? And how long would I survive down there on my own?

Flying over mountains reminds us how fragile our lives are. You will be dead soon! And, brother, so will I. But when we're flying high through darkening skies it feels like our dreams might just survive, survive, survive . . .

AWESOME!

Videoconferencing your parents and seeing more than just their foreheads

Do you get the forehead hello?

That's how my dad answers video calls.

I see the corner of his head and the pink light fixture in the **popcorn ceiling** with my mom's white hair poking out the side.

On one hand you would think a thousand video calls would help him figure out how to hold the phone. On the other it's sweet seeing a few wispy gray strands of his hair and hearing his warm smile a couple seconds before seeing it.

We live in an unimaginable future.

Strapping ourselves inside metal tubes and flying across the world we land and press buttons to beam smiling faces through satellites in outer space just to instantly connect hearts and say, "I love you."

I remember the day I visited my parents in the house I grew up in and showed my dad my first smartphone. He shook his head and said, "It's like the whole world in your hand!"

Now he has one, too.

We connect from far away.

Texts are fine, calls are good, grandma hair is great.

And when he eventually holds his hand in front of him and I see his thick glasses and spotted face shining back?

Well, that is most definitely

AWESOME!

The first warm day of spring

I went to school in a small town on a big lake.

Sharp winter air bit our cheeks as we skidded across **slippery slush sidewalks** under sweaty bundles of wet scarves and snow-covered hats. Fingers froze and so did toes during our red-faced races to class.

Basically, it was all about getting where you were going and then staying there for good. After all, once you slow-peeled off all those steamy layers, you never felt like moving again. Couch sessions were common with video games, **basement movies**, and dialing for dinner part of the hibernation preservation.

We were grizzlies in the den until those winter chills faded into those warm breezes of the first day of spring! That's when warm air finally blew across our faces and woke up our senses.

Tiny leaves push through **sandy sidewalk cracks** reaching out like skinny fists to the heavens. Warm winds stir up heady smells of dark topsoil, flower pollen, and crispy sun-dried worms. Running shoes soak through yellow grass and **tiny mud bubbles** rise around every step as you artfully dodge dirty-ice chunks in the shade and last year's dog poo.

Bike helmets wobble on shaky bikes, tongue-wagging dogs go on street-strolling hikes, and everyone smiles at this moment of delight. So lose the jacket and get on your feet! Come join the party in the street! Just smell the trees and sniff those blossoms! Because the first warm day of spring is completely

AWESOME!

When someone you haven't seen in years suddenly pops into one of your dreams

....

My friend Chris took his own life years ago.

I revisit his memory as best I can, but the truth is he's slowly slipping away. I sometimes write on his old **maroon fuzzy blanket** and I keep his broken-spined copy of *Maus* on my shelf, but his voice, his laugh, his mannerisms—they're all fading. I'm losing his essence. Just like my family and friends will one day lose mine.

A couple times a year, something magical happens and Chris suddenly shows up in my dreams. He's there! He's alive! He's well! And although sometimes I can barely remember what happened in the dream, when I wake up I feel that same sense of love I felt at the end of long days together at school.

When I wake up from a **Surprise Cameo Dream**, I try to stay still in my bed to savor the moment as long as possible. I know those warm memories won't last, so I have to soak them in.

Whether it's a lost crush from years ago, an old boss back at the restaurant, or maybe your dad suddenly serving you breakfast again at the kitchen table . . . let's enjoy the visitors who come back for a cameo and enjoy our dreams taking us through twisty mental tunnels to deliver us back to deeply real feelings of love.

AWESOME!

Remembering we're all pretty much the same

We're all pretty much the same.

Packed tightly in our **skintight skin** is a bumpy clump of slippery organs and brittle bones. Yes, you're a pile of bones, I'm a bucket of blood, you're a slab of muscle, I'm a chunk of chub. And no matter what we got squeezing through our veins, **zooming through our brains**, and dripping out our drains, one big thing just always remains.

We're all pretty much the same.

We're all pretty much the same.

We're all pretty much the same.

Baby brains buzz and little eardrums pop—pop!—**baby lungs breathe deep** and little eyelids flop—flop!—but as we grow up and grow older, we let differences become our guide, we start choosing our own adventures, we start carving paths and curving wide. We settle into ourselves, **settle into our skin**, settle into our lives, and find comforts within . . .

We grow up, we grow older, **some grow hotter**, some grow colder. We focus on our tastes, on our preferences and choices, we find our kinds of friends, we read our kinds of voices. We might cut deep paths, **we may turn others away**, we may deepen our divides, we might have nothing nice to say.

But way down deep in our stomachs, way down deep in our

hearts, we can remember no matter which way we turn, **which lessons we learn**, which bridges we burn . . .

We're all pretty much the same.

We're all pretty much the same.

No matter what money we earn, **what chances we churn**, what choices we spurn . . .

We're all pretty much the same.

We're all pretty much the same.

Yes, we've all got cracks and chips, **we've all got sores and scratches**, we've all got doubts and dreams, we've all got hearts with patches. We laugh and cry, we soar and sink, we zoom up and down, we stop and think.

I'm saying behind your favorite things, behind your best best friends, behind your fears and doubts . . . we'll be waiting here again.

We're all in this big show together.

We're all singing the same song.

We're all living for today and tomorrow.

So may we all keep holding on.

AWESOME!

That dirty melting snowman across the street suddenly reflecting back to you a strangely poignant metaphor about life itself

....

One twig arm sagging loosely and the other lying on the melting snow and wet yellow grass below. Carrot nose chewed up by a squirrel. Torso about to fall out. Head about to fall off.

We're not here long. And even if we come back we probably won't remember this. This is rare. This is special. This is something.

Thank you for hanging out again.

Thank you for another great conversation.

Thank you for sharing your love.

And thank you for being truly

AWESOME!

The day that giant pimple finally disappears · Holding your driver's license for the first time · When the teacher hands back your test and says, "Good job" · When the bell curve saves you · When the cat helps you find your keys · Watching a dog eat peanut butter · When your pet falls asleep on you · When the free Wi-Fi doesn't require a log-in · When your phone is about to die and a stranger saves you with their power cord · Feeling like Han Solo in hyperdrive when you flip your high beams on during a snowfall · Watching all the letters flip at an old train station · Taking a shot of whipped cream from the can when no one's looking · The moment you discover the free bread at the restaurant is warm · When the garbage truck goes past your house blaring "Roxanne" by The Police at full volume · Sneaking out of the house late at night just to admire a full moon · Sitting with your grandma at the piano and teaching her how to play "Chopsticks" for the first time · When you expect a bad mark but end up with a good mark · When you come home after a cold day of school and just take a long bubble bath · Eating the part of the cookie that fell in the milk · Having to buy bigger shirts because working out has caused the old shirts to get too tight around the arms and chest · That moment when your sinuses feel completely clear right after a big sneeze · Finding your favorite shirt that you forgot about at your friend's house · Your grandma's basement · Completing the video game level you've been working on for days · When the power comes back on after a sudden blackout · Gutting a pumpkin with your bare hands · The smell of the baseball card touching that dry stick of bubble gum after you unwrap them from that waxy wrapping paper · Shaving your legs then jumping in a cold pool · Being the first person in the house to tear off the film over a new container of butter and sticking your knife in virgin territory · Screaming at the TV when you disagree · Typing in the correct website address before the wrong one loads · Finally finding that super tiny piece of LEGO after searching and searching the bottom of that giant Tupperware container of like a million pieces · Hearing your teenage son's voice crackling and for the first time realizing he's becoming a man · When you don't have to spend two days cleaning the muffin tray because the muffins you baked came out of the baking tray in one piece • Playing hide and seek in the dark at the end of the party • Picking all the M&M's out of the trail mix • Being small enough to hide in a kitchen cupboard • Getting licked by a rabbit • When the pothole you run over every day is finally filled in and smooth • Short basketball players • When there's just enough milk in the carton for your first morning cup of coffee • When you open the bathroom door after a steaming hot shower and you get that cool blast of air and feel all clean and refreshed • Drinking out of a fancy glass with your pinkie up in the air • Actually catching the popcorn in your mouth • When you open a can of cranberry sauce and it falls out in the shape of the can • The soft insides of a brand new sweatshirt • Humming the *Rocky* theme song whenever you're running up a long flight of stairs • Getting a foot rub without asking for one • A ponytail or bun that stays perfectly composed without a single strand escaping • Looking at the northern lights while lying in a wheat field • The moment after you wake up but before your kids wake up • When you open your eyes in the morning and can tell by the color of the light in the room that it snowed last night • When the cars around you change lanes at the same time like a car ballet • Listening to "The Imperial March" from *Star Wars* on your headphones while walking around in public • When you and someone else in the parking lot hit the "lock-lock" sequence so both cars beep in unison • Driving on a highway at full speed while everyone going the other way is completely backed up • Using a baby spoon to eat pudding so it lasts longer • When a cat rubs up against your freshly shaven legs • Walking on top of a crispy layer of snow and not falling through • Eating cherry tomatoes fresh out of the garden • Opening a bag of dill pickle crisps and the glands in your cheeks start tingling with anticipation • Winning a ridiculous five-foot-tall karate trophy • The smell of an Aussie summer with the ocean and your favorite sun tan cream and the warmth of the sun on your face and a small breeze in the air • When you're a waiter and somebody leaves you a really big tip • Jumping on a trampoline and keeping your shoes on so there is more grippiness and your jumps are less wasted • Old lady jewelry for a quarter at yard sales • The smell g champa leaves behind after it's done burning • Finding all the potato chips in the bag that are folded over • Houses with secret doors or secret rooms • The first bite into your favorite sushi roll along with a glass of chilled Pinot Grigio • Faking sickness so you don't have to go to school • The last day of a snowboarding vacation on the last lift up the mountain and sitting at the peak with your friends looking over the scenery and knowing it'll be another year until you get to do this again • Hearing your kids say, "Hi daddy!" on the phone in the middle of your workday • Letting your dog sleep with you even though he snores and farts all night • Lying down in the snow in one of those full-body snowsuits you had as a kid and just feeling so warm in that warm cushiony snow • Catching someone checking you out • Discovering someone who loves the same obscure band that you do • When kids show you a sore on their middle finger and they just hold up that finger not knowing what it means • Seeing an old man with a long white beard dressed as Santa jogging down the street in the middle of July • When your mom sits too far back in a banana chair, falls over, and can't get up • Racking up good traffic karma by letting trucks merge in front of you on the highway and then speeding past a traffic cop later and nothing happens • That one huge exploding firework that covers the whole sky • When the hold music at the pharmacy somehow hits you right in the heart • Blue and yellow and pink and gold wildflowers in the sewer drain ditch beside the country highway • Cannonballing into the pool • Finding one last tea bag in that box you thought was empty • Falling asleep to the sound of crickets • Clothes pegs as an invention • That one guy who cracks loud jokes in the two seconds of silence between previews in the dark and packed movie theater • Police letting you off with a warning and then going home and eating frozen mint girl scout cookies • When you thought you lost your glasses and then find them on the top of your head • Eating lobster or crab and removing that perfectly shaped claw • The look on a kid's face when he's watching balloon animals being made • No-questions-asked return policies • When restaurants put ice in the urinal

Seeing the lightbulb come on for a kid learning to read · Pulling fresh cotton balls apart · The sound of a can of beer opening · Being chosen from the audience to go onstage and be part of the magic trick · Watching a film for two hours without any inclination of the twist at the end and then having the hairs on the back of your neck stand up and thinking about it for days after · When you've got little kids and your partner takes them out for the morning so you can have a long sleep-in and you hear them saying, "Be quiet, don't wake mommy" right before you fall back asleep · New shoes when you're five · Finding a glass of water on the bedside table and chugging it in the middle of the night so you wake up with no hangover · The sound of sharp skates on a fresh sheet of ice · Watching home movies of Christmas past · The liberating feeling of sleeping naked · Watching every single installment of a film series in one day · Finding that chip in the bag that's got the most seasonings · Walking around barefoot all day while camping or at the beach and then finally washing and drying your feet and putting on socks and shoes · When you've had the longest, most stressful, exhausting day ever and the last thing you feel like doing is cooking dinner, and you walk in the door and someone says to you, "I just ordered takeout, it'll be here in ten minutes" · When you're waiting for a bus at a bus stop and you're standing like five feet past the stop but the bus still somehow pulls up and opens its doors right in front of you · Getting ready for a night out on da town · Finishing a crossword puzzle without cheating · Getting a raise when you didn't ask for one and when it's not an annual thing and when your boss just says you deserve it · The beginning of being in love when you can't go five minutes without talking to each other and everything else in your life suddenly seems less important · The really old Rudolph movie where the characters are made out of modeling clay or something · Waking up from a nap in a panic at college because you're late for your next class only to realize this is the one day a week you don't have any classes · Finally getting that sneeze out you've been waiting for all day · Talking and laughing and joking in bed after having sex · The overly expressive faces of small children especially when they're pouting or surprised · When stuff smells like where you were last time you were having a good time · Singing along to a song even when you don't know the words · Doing a trick on your skateboard you haven't tried in a while and landing it · Scratch-and-sniff stickers · When you finally get the words right to the fast part of a song · Squeezing under an umbrella with a stranger · Commenting about something during class and getting that deep "Ooooooooooh" from your professor · The sound of your dog's collar jingling as he comes running to meet you at the front door · Waking up to the sound of rain in the middle of the night especially when you live in South Carolina · When an illuminated sign has a few blown bulbs and the remaining letters make a dirty word · Deleting hundreds of unopened junk emails simultaneously · When the medicine you took an hour ago finally kicks in · Finding out that someone you have the hots for has them for you, too · Getting an unexpected hug, kiss, or butt slap from your significant other after years of being together · Calling shotgun for the long car trip · Paying all the bills and having money left over · Entering a warm building after freezing outside · Opening the pickle jar on your first try · Little birds chasing big birds · The ability to walk · A whole day by yourself to read · Turning the vent on an electric hand dryer upward · Finally figuring out one of those confusing metal puzzle games · Sticking your hands in any kind of dough and squeezing it through your fingers · Finding a bird's nest with eggs in it and suddenly feeling like you want to guard it · The look of anticipation in someone's eyes before you kiss them for the first time · Hearing the mail slot open and the mail drop onto your front tiles · Trying on your new clothes as soon as you get back from the mall · The feeling after that perfect shot during a round of golf that makes you forget all the bad shots before · Leaving a store to realize that your car was towed because you accidentally parked in a tow-away zone and then realizing a minute later that some anonymous tow truck driver just moved your car around the corner and onto a side street, thus saving you a $400 fine · That big morning stretch that loosens your whole body and makes you want to sleep again · Poutine and beer at a dark bar · Dancing in the rain and not the light rain but the kind that leaves your hair and clothes completely drenched and makes you feel like you're a part of nature · Cracking every knuckle on your hand at once · Successful communication between two people who speak absolutely none of each other's language · Lying on an old saggy sofa or mattress that molds perfectly around you like a pillowy hug · When your girlfriend smells like a freshly ironed shirt · Being the oldest guy at the arcade · A good truck stop on a long road trip · Swimming naked · Paying for the food of the guy behind you at a fast-food joint · The first drink of water after waking up from a late night out when your mouth is really dry and pasty · Singing "Sweet Caroline" at the top of your lungs at Fenway Park on a warm sunny day with 35,000 rowdy happy fans · Hitting that point in the late night where everyone decides to just stay up for the sunrise and there's this really raw energy in the room · Finding a pair of pants that fit you the right way and you feel so confident in them · The *TINK* you hear when hitting a golf ball with a driver and knowing you got it just right · When you order fries and they make a fresh batch · The fact that jellyfish have been on earth for 250 million years before even dinosaurs got here · Washing your hair in the rain · When someone makes your bed for you · Skipping rocks on a quiet morning at a calm lake · Finding a long-lost childhood toy that's been hiding under several boxes in the basement · When your limbs feel like jelly after a really tough workout · Chasing your giggling mom with the vacuum cleaner · Driving through a deep puddle at a good clip · Getting the cast off after six long weeks · Getting bagels that are still hot from the oven · Being completely care-free · Cuddling in bed when you are cold and your bedmate is really warm · See-ing your parents flirt · Keeping all the cotton balls from the tops of medicine bottles and never having to buy cotton balls · When you hit the cart that picks up the golf balls at the driving range · When February has 28 days and starts on a Sunday and the calendar looks neat and square · Winking at someone and them completely understanding what to do · When a storm knocks the power out for a while but you can still read by rain-storm-daylight or emergency-candle light in the midst of that eerie, non-buzzy quiet · Finally getting that sneeze out that's been stuck all day · Somehow correctly guessing your old password while logging into a website you haven't used in forever · When it's your birth-day on a school day and your name is on the announcements · When you're at a concert and the band is between songs and someone at the back yells out "FREEEEEBIRRRRD!!!" · Walking on a skinny curb pretending you're on a tight-rope · Celebrating your half-birthday · Farting in the bathtub · Seeing the first bird at the feeder · Leaving your house really late and somehow still getting there on time · When you're on the ellip-tical at the gym and you and the person next to you suddenly start synchroniz-ing your "ellipses" and then you look at each other and smile · Turning off the open sign at the end of a double shift · Finding a typo in a boook · When a newborn with its eyes closed suddenly grasps your baby finger with their hand · When the bus driver lets you on the bus even though you forgot your ticket · Peeling really sticky tape or that blue tacky stuff off your wall and not having any of your dorm room paint come off with it · When someone finally suggests the perfect nickname for your first car · When at the end of a really long week at uni the lecturer comes in and asks everyone to take out a blank sheet of paper and write down a list of things you enjoy doing together with the last time you remember doing that thing and then suddenly lets everyone off two hours early to go do one of those things · The first time you successfully climb up the slide · Smelling your favorite laundry detergent on someone else · When a butterfly lands on you · A long awkward silence followed by everyone laughing · That one person who mixes all their flavors together at the soda fountain and insists to everyone back at the turny-chairs that it really does taste great · When someone jumps into the song you're singing and adds the harmony · Warm photocopies · When you're in your seventies and you somehow run into your long-lost childhood best friend while traveling in another country · When you finally confess to someone special that horrible thing about you and they don't pull away · Biking somewhere you were just about to drive · Finally finding underwear that is comfortable and fits you perfectly and deciding to just buy it forever · Calling someone and it rings three times and you're getting ready to leave a voicemail and then they suddenly pick up · When the "delivered" notification pops up under the text and you see the three dots pop up right away · Sitting on the city bus in the high-occupancy lane while zooming past all the cars right beside you in a traffic jam · Fingertip touching and extended eye contact · Successfully guessing if that accent is Australian, British, or South African · Finding that perfect spot to build your sandcastle with the ideal wet-dry sand consistency and yet still out of range of the waves · When they write another book in a really good series you thought was over · Reading a book about awesome things and then making your own list

OUR BOOK OF

AWESOME

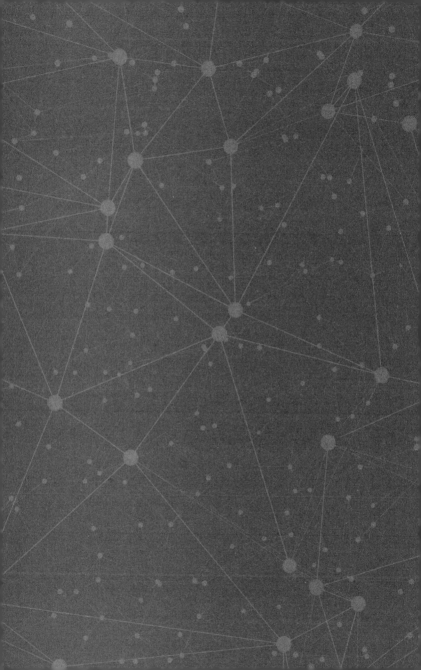

OUR BOOK OF

AWESOME

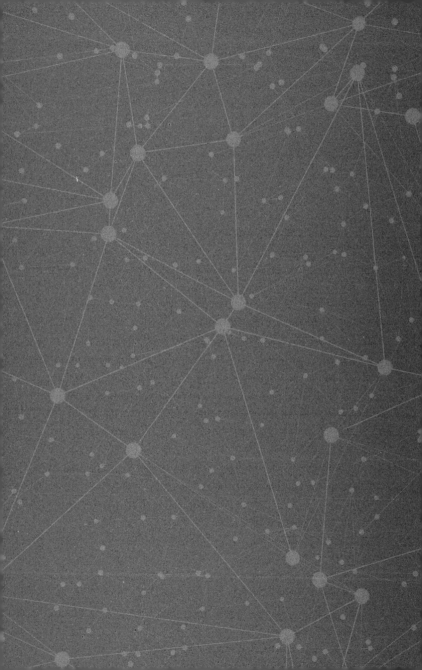

OUR BOOK OF

AWESOME

OUR BOOK OF

AWESOME